Enlighten Up!

An Educator's Guide to Stress-Free Living

Lynell Burmark • Lou Fournier

Association for Supervision and Curriculum Development
Alexandria, Virginia USA

Association for Supervision and Curriculum Development
1703 N. Beauregard St. • Alexandria, VA 22311-1714 USA
Telephone: 800-933-2723 or 703-578-9600 • Fax: 703-575-5400
Web site: http://www.ascd.org • E-mail: member@ascd.org

Gene R. Carter, *Executive Director;* Nancy Modrak, *Director of Publishing;* Julie Houtz, *Director of Book Editing & Production;* Ernesto Yermoli, *Project Manager;* Shelley Young, *Senior Graphic Designer;* BMWW, *Typesetter.*

Printed in the United States of America.

April 2003 sale book.

ISBN: 0-87120-758-3 ASCD product no.: 102106 ASCD member price: $15.95 nonmember price: $18.95

Library of Congress Cataloging-in-Publication Data

Burmark, Lynell, 1946–
Enlighten up! : an educator's guide to stress-free living / Lynell Burmark and Lou Fournier.
p. cm.
ISBN 0-87120-758-3 (alk. paper)
1. Teachers—Job stress—Handbooks, manuals, etc. 2. Teachers—Conduct of life—Handbooks, manuals. I. Fournier, Lou. II. Title

LB2333.3.B87 2003
371.1′01′9—dc21 2003001414

12 11 10 09 08 07 06 05 04 03 12 11 10 9 8 7 6 5 4 3 2 1

Table of Contents

Foreword

This well-researched, well-written, and engaging book is like having a friendly personal helpmate. Instead of offering the usual "reasons" for stress-related problems, the authors show us how to recontextualize and resolve them. The simple but helpful exercises and technologies described in the book are surprisingly effective because they are based on the most advanced research about the basic qualities that underlie all human thought and emotion.

Whereas most books devoted to enhancing life skills are limited to content only, *Enlighten Up!* constitutes a more advanced approach to the subject. For instance, the authors clearly emphasize the importance of overall context, as illustrated by the personal vignettes that make the writing interesting and personal and not just didactic.

Although addressed to educators, this concise gem of a book is a valuable resource for anyone who is interested in more pleasurable, satisfying, and effective living.

—David R. Hawkins

Preface

Books on stress are about as ubiquitous as the phenomenon itself. Generally they fall into two broad categories: scientific and subjective.

Authors approaching the topic of stress from a scientific perspective present only information that meets the ostensibly objective criteria of reproducible results, hard facts, longitudinal studies, and coldly measurable data: the findings of allopathic medicine, for example, or clinical psychology. Science has profoundly broadened our understanding of the physiology and psychology of stress, and provides us with a steady frame of reference against which to measure and balance what we read in more subjective books on the subject.

By subjective we mean books that, though typically based on the strict findings of science, also offer extensive personal observations in the form of subjective interpretations and informed speculation on what all that hard research means. Sometimes the authors of such books are well-regarded scientists who manage to find broad public acceptance by discussing their personal interpretations in nonacademic language—scholars and physicians such as Mihaly Csikszentmihalyi and Susan Lark. In other instances, authors working outside of academia manage to so engagingly hit a nerve with the public that their speculations become bestsellers, such as in the cases of Wayne Dyer and Richard Bolles.

Authors of scientific books on stress are typically respectful of the subjective approach, and vice versa. Scientists who don't feel the need to be dogmatic about the scientific method will commonly make supportive comments about speculative writings, while still warning us that such material is subjective and cannot be proven scientifically. Similarly, subjective writers are almost always highly supportive of the contributions of science, though they still caution that scientific data are limited by the hard, subjective boundaries of presumed fact and methodologies.

We wrote this book hoping to bridge the scientific and subjective worlds. Lynell is a lifelong academic with four degrees and a distinguished career in education; Lou is a lifelong trainer in human potential development and an accomplished writer. Reflecting our backgrounds, we chose to view the scientific and subjective perspectives as complementary rather than confrontational. We agreed that both approaches have much to offer, so long as each is appropriately identified, and have employed both in the following pages. In places, we even discuss the extremes of each perspective: physiological research unadorned by interpretation on the one hand, and the most daring subjective research being done today on the other.

Introduction

Few would challenge the notion that in an ideal world it would be possible to live stress-free. We believe it's possible to do so even in the world as it exists today, since living an ideal has much more to do with what goes on inside us than with what goes on outside. That, essentially, is the primary message of this book.

This is not a book on stress management—a point on which we elaborate in Chapter 9 (and one that we can't "stress" enough). Rather, this is a book about resourcefulness. It is different from books you may have already encountered on stress in two main ways: it significantly redefines the term, and it offers realistic hope and comfort to all who struggle with this seemingly inescapable condition. Our book touches on the commonly cited antidotes for stress in stress-management circles, such as time management, diet, exercise, and the like, but only long enough to acknowledge that these things clearly play a role in optimal well-being. These methods make great fish, already caught and ready to eat, but we're much more concerned with *learning* to fish—and on a deeper level, learning to find fish you never knew were out there, particularly when it seems that your favorite fishing holes have become watery ghost towns.

Of course, we owe much to the best explorers of the inner path, especially those who managed to combine far-reaching new insights with pragmatic simplicity for maximum accessibility by their readers—a model to which we too are committed. Although the ability to tap into resources that once seemed beyond our reach may seem too pie-in-the-sky for people in the crush of practical exigencies, you will see in this book that it is not.

We begin our discussion with a fresh understanding of what stress feels like and explore such issues as locus of control and the demands of change. We examine how the contemporary work ethic has come to embrace a perverse standard of relentless labor, and we share medical research on the shocking cost of "overachieving." Time and its presumed pressures are also considered as we contemplate the difference between flow and frenzy. We take a look at the deeper significance of clutter and offer practical tips on how to deal with money and bring more of it into our personal and professional lives. For all who may have thought the world would be a great place if it weren't for the people, we consider the nature and significance of relationships. We demonstrate that everything around us is in vibratory motion, and what this means in terms of how music, words, and even the physical human heart affect us at the deepest levels. Finally, we explore the true meaning of power and purpose and invite our readers to "enlighten up" because, in the end, there is no such thing as stress.

1

The Wake-Up Call

What were your first thoughts when you woke up this morning? Perhaps one of these crossed your dimly dawning consciousness:

- "Ahhh, thank God it's morning! I can hardly wait to get to work."
- "I'd almost like to skip my 5-mile run so I could get there sooner."
- "Mmmm, glad I went to the store last night to pick up the barley greens, wheat grass, and alfalfa powder for my invigorating morning breakfast drink."
- "Whose bright idea was it to set the alarm?"
- "You know, there's a reason they call it work."
- "If only my job weren't so *stressful*."

So you think *your* job is stressful? Consider a job that could easily keep several people busy for some 70 hours a week, holds you responsible for work while constantly questioning your authority, and expects you magically to change the lives of countless people for the better, often with little support from the community or your bosses. What? That *is* your job? Oh, so you're an educator.

Stress: The Tension Between Our Expectations and Our Resources

An educator's day is most certainly a challenge. But whether we feel anxiety or gleeful anticipation reveals less about the day's events than it does about what we expect of ourselves. We see our lives through our expectations, which are generally both too high and too low: although we expect to be able to accomplish more, better, and faster, we typically think our capabilities to do so are insufficient. The result of this contradictory self-view is the restrictive, exhausting sense that we loosely call "stress."

Stress is the sense that our options, our available internal resources, are too limited for the particular challenges we face. In the most stressful situations, we can sense our options actually decreasing by the moment, confining us ever more tightly to the realm of frustration and helplessness. And it's all too easy to take this frustration personally, as though life were directing this solitary confinement pointedly at us. This sentiment is revealed in such ubiquitous avowals of resignation as "What are you gonna do?" "Wouldn't you know it?" "What else could you expect?" and so on.

Yet we need not resign ourselves to fatalism. Murphy's Law, which states that "anything that *can* go wrong *will* go wrong," can be repealed. Stress is illusory, and we have it within us to control the illusion—and with it, our lives.

Speaking of control, don't you just hate the term "control freak," especially when someone mistakes you for one? Still, we all want to be in control of our lives. In fact, one of the more common symptoms of stress is the sense of losing control. There is, however, a big difference between control and knowing how to tap into previously unknown internal resources. Let's take a closer look at this distinction.

Locus of Control

In our workshops, we often play the 1960s hit, "My Elusive Dreams."[1] The lyrics describe a young man who travels from place to disappointing place, endlessly, hopelessly pursuing his ephemeral dreams.

As more than one of our workshops' participants have pointed out, the problem is that the song's narrator has placed the locus of control for his happiness outside himself. Look at some of the expressions we use when confronted with what seems to be our own inner helplessness: "You got me." "How would I know?" "It's beyond me." Well, if we feel we can't possibly know, then we can easily feel that we have no choice but to look beyond the borders of ourselves to externals. How many times have you heard or thought something like "That new policy makes me crazy!" or "That student almost made me quit today"? In our workshops, we like to ask participants to conduct the exercise in Figure 1.1.

1.1 Pause and Apply

Think for a few minutes about how you would fill in the blanks in this sentence:

"__________ makes (or made) me __________."

We have noticed that most of our workshop participants tend to generate sentences that are either neutral ("Coffee makes me wake up") or negative ("Standardized tests make me crazy"). Of course, positive comments are possible as well; one of the most pleasant we've heard is "My students make me smile." But even with the positive responses, we are reacting to external forces rather than exercising our own internal power. (English teachers will recognize that in these sentences, the speaker is the *object* rather than the *subject* of the verb.)

Inner vs. Outer Control

By placing the locus of control outside of ourselves, we ensure that we will *never* be in control. So long as we allow indeterminate forces to run our lives at their whim, our lives can never really be our own. We hasten to add that it's possible to overcompensate for this realization; some people think, "Oh, okay, then all my answers are within me. I just need to look within, and I'll find everything I need." This is a pleasant and even comforting thought, and a mantra of a lot of New Age literature, but it's more than a little misleading. *Not all answers are within us*. By looking too narrowly inward we risk disregarding the fact that life is a systemic experience. Some of the most important lessons we learn occur through external circumstances—through the impact of others on our lives, and through our openness to discerning the significance of seeming obstacles that confront us.

It's easy to get frustrated when we sense that we can't control our lives, but it isn't control that we need. What we really need are resources. The paradox here is that we already have far more resources within us than we recognize—all those resources that we don't see when we are under stress. This is true at any given moment of our lives, regardless of how resourceful we already think or don't think we are.

We might compare our tumultuous lives to whitewater rafting (an adventure not unlike an educator's typical day!). If you're new and inexperienced with whitewater rapids, you feel terrified and overwhelmed; if you're experienced and well trained, however, the same circumstances bring out a sense of excitement and confidence. There is often a fine line between fear and excitement, and resourcefulness allows us to cross it.

When we feel overwhelmed, our immediate reflex is to clutch desperately for control; it seems to be the only way to stop the sense of helplessness. Ironically, in such situations, that reflex usually leads to even greater loss of control. On the other hand, when we know because of our experience and training that we have the resources to deal with a challenge, we don't need to struggle for control. There is nothing *to* control; we simply ride the currents and go with the flow.

A mind in flow "seems to be the result of total concentration on a doable task, which can be physical, intellectual, or even emotional," says Mihaly Csikszentmihalyi, psychologist and author of the 1991 book *Flow: The Psychology of Optimal Experience*.[2] He elaborates:

> Sports psychologists recognized that athletes describing how they felt when they were at their best sounded very much as if they'd been in flow. So why should a blissed-out state of mind enhance performance? The key is in the type and amount of attention the athlete pays to the task. In a series of studies, sports scientists at Arizona State University have looked at the brain waves of archers, shooters, and golfers in the seconds before they release a motion. The researchers found decreases in activity in the left hemisphere of the brain, the hemisphere thought to handle rational thought. The decline in left-hemisphere activity represents less attention to the mechanics of the action and more on how it feels. And only certain ratios of left-to-right-hemisphere activity correlate with peak performance, suggesting that there is an ideal frame of mind.[3]

Classroom teachers most often witness the "flow" frame of mind when they engage teams of students in project-based learning. When students are committed to a clear goal, teachers no longer have to worry about "time on task" or other methods of enforcing classroom discipline, and can concern themselves instead with finding staff to keep the computer lab open before and after school so that students can continue to work on their projects!

Prescriptions for Control

In their book *Out of Its Mind: Psychiatry in Crisis—A Call for Reform*, authors J. Allan Hobson and Jonathan Leonard lament American psychiatry's unholy devotion to tranquilizers. They point out that by the 1980s and '90s, cost-conscious insurance companies had figured out that drugs were cheaper than therapy, so they redefined mental health care as a kind of pharmacological outpatient service (our term, not theirs). Even when insurance companies do pay for therapy, they only allow a limited number of sessions at an approved hourly rate, which covers only the fees of psychologists and social workers rather than those of more expensive psychiatrists.[4]

It's not only insurance companies that encourage consumers to seek pharmaceutical solutions to life's problems. Pharmaceutical companies themselves are now running two-page advertisements that explain why at least 20 million Americans should consider seeing their doctor about a quick fix for fatigue, anxiety, and—well, for just not feeling quite like yourself. In fact, prescription tranquilizers are another example of our tendency to place the locus of control outside ourselves: many doctors and pharmaceutical companies would have us believe that we need put no more effort into changing our state of mind than popping a "happy pill."

Nowadays, more and more happy pills are available even without a prescription. According to the Life Extension Foundation (LEF), one of the best-selling dietary supplements in the United States today is SAMe (pronounced "Sammy").[5] SAMe (s-adenosylmethionine) is so popular because most depressed people who try this "natural approach" feel better and reorder it, in spite of the cost. When SAMe was first introduced in 1996, Americans were importing it from Italy at $45 per 3-day supply. Mail-order companies like LEF now offer the drug at substantial savings, but it's still significantly more expensive than herbal mood enhancers like St. John's Wort or 5-HTP.

Though not all articles or sales brochures on SAMe bother to mention it, the supplement can cause homocysteine buildup. According to the American Heart Association, "epidemiological studies have shown that too much homocysteine in the blood is related to a higher risk of coronary heart disease, stroke, and peripheral vascular disease."[6] You might as well be in a good mood while you're playing Russian roulette with heart attacks and strokes! One responsible online vendor of SAMe advises complementing it with Vitamin B-complex to prevent homocysteine buildup and avoid B-complex deficiency, which itself is "often enough to cause low mood."[7]

Depression and Stress

Depression is a most serious matter. Daniel G. Amen, author of *Change Your Brain, Change Your Life*, stated in a recent radio interview that 49 percent of Americans will have a diagnosable psychiatric disorder in their lifetimes. The most common disorders, he stated, are anxiety, depression, and substance abuse.[8]

Susan M. Lark, Stanford University Medical School professor and authority in the fields of clinical nutrition and preventive medicine, warns us that "depressive disorders have a greater effect on physical and social functioning, body pain, and overall health than diabetes, arthritis, and even heart disease. By the year 2020, depression is estimated to be the second-leading cause of disability in the world."[9] According to Dr. Lark, regardless of the cause of their depression, most depressed people have one thing in common: low levels of the neurotransmitter serotonin, the body's own mood-altering drug, which "helps people cope with stress."[10]

If you are depressed, you can't handle stress. And if you internalize stress, you become depressed. Once you get on this treadmill, is there any way off? Don't worry; we'll get to that. In the meantime, a little B-complex couldn't hurt.

Who Scrambled My Eggs?

When we are already under stress, small pressures—a child misbehaving in class, a budget report due to the district, another meeting running past dinnertime—can be enough to drive us over the edge. We've all witnessed it: in a restaurant, a customer blows up and screams at the waitress, "Who scrambled my eggs? I ordered them sunny-side up!" As detached observers with fluffy Belgian waffles and crisp bacon on our plates, we can see that the customer's reaction is clearly out of proportion to the offense.

Of course, the anger has less to do with eggs than it does with running out of stress-busting resources. And the fastest way to exhaust that resource supply—short of a series of traumatic events—is to live a life full of changes. We love this invitation from our Thornburg Center colleague, Bernajean Porter: "Change is good. You go first."

Of course, some change *is* good: two tens for a five, two twenties for a ten, the coins from a winning slot machine. We personally have found a change of hair to be quick, easy, and exhilarating: Lou has the baseball cap with the fake ponytail hanging down the back; Lynell has the golf cap with hot-pink tresses, complemented by sunglasses with an attitude. We may have staff meetings to attend, but we don't have to go with a bald spot or dishwater-blond hair.

Unfortunately, most changes in life aren't as simple as plopping on a hair-enhancing hat. Let's face it: learning new skills, procedures, and ways of thinking takes work, especially in the beginning stages. This can be graphically illustrated by the infamous sigmoid curve (Figure 1.2). At the most basic level, this S-curve describes the biological life cycle: we're born; we struggle and cry, crawl and stumble, and eventually make a pretty good run for it; then we peak, slow down, decline, and die.

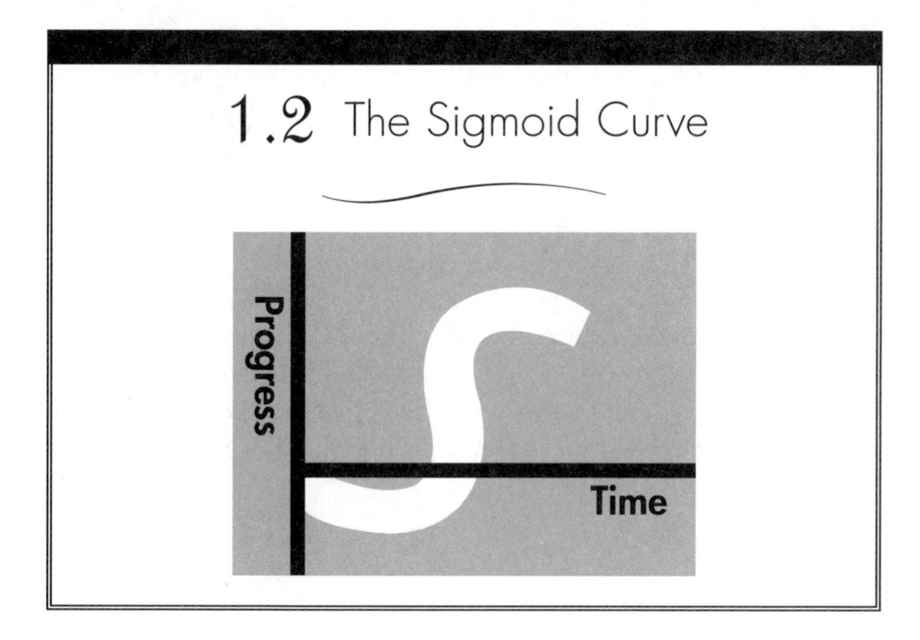

1.2 The Sigmoid Curve

In his landmark 1994 book *The Age of Paradox,*[11] management guru Charles Handy was the first to apply the S-curve life cycle to organizations. As he explains it, every new S-curve begins with a slight, negative dip representing the stage at which the effort is so great that you wonder if the enterprise will ever get off the ground. Consider the S-curve of new teachers coming into the school system. Not only do they have to meet the needs of a diverse student population, but they also have to figure out all the procedures (many of which seem conceived without logic and sustained without purpose), the politics, the culture, the dress codes, the phones, the computer network, the promotions policy, the parent conferences, the special services—the list goes on. In addition, Murphy would argue, the things that *do* seem to make sense are the most likely to be changed.

Talk about a roller-coaster ride! Life these days is just one S-curve after another, with barely enough time to ride the peak before nosediving into the next valley. While some people would give the shirt off their back for the thrill of the ride, others would only give their lunch.

The ATM Also Accepts Deposits

The challenge with S-curves is the same one we face with our checkbooks: to keep things in balance, we need resources or deposits.

Some years back, Lynell was talking to a wealthy friend about how so many people never seem to have quite enough money. The friend's five-year-old son piped up: "Oh, that's not a problem. You just do what my mom does. You go to the bank, and they give you all the money you ask for!"

His big brown eyes grew larger by the moment as Lynell explained that his daddy put the money *in* so that it would be there for his mommy to take it *out*!

It's not only our monetary savings that need income to balance outgo. We all have emotional and psychological personal "bank accounts" from which we make frequent withdrawals every day. These need deposits as well, and, happily, they're easy and very rewarding to make. Use the exercise in Figure 1.3 to jot down some things that you can do for yourself to ensure that your account is never overdrawn. We've started you off with an example.

1.3 Pause and Apply

Deposits to Make to My Account	
Date	**Deposit**
October 2	Begin new exercise regimen.

Did you list your own staff development? Remember that course you've been meaning to take on using the Internet? What about that pledge to walk three times a week during your lunch break? And that music CD that you find so relaxing: can you buy a second copy to have at work? Share your list with a colleague and see it as a growing account. Think of the deposits as the resources you'll need for those inevitable dips in the S-curve. And remember: you can't withdraw until you deposit.

Constants vs. Change

We learned from our friend Richard Bolles (author of *What Color Is Your Parachute?*) that change is only one end of a continuum that also includes constants. Take a moment to fill in the chart in Figure 1.4 (or use a separate piece of paper). List your blessings—the things you know you can count on to remain constant in your life—on the left, and your opportunities—things that you'd like to see change for the better—on the right.

1.4 Pause and Apply

Constants (blessings)	Change (opportunities)
Things I'm thankful for:	Things I wish were different:
•	•
•	•
•	•
•	•
•	•
•	•
•	•
•	•
•	•
•	•

Now look at your list of blessings. Constants are the things that remain in our lives no matter what goes on around or within us; they give us a sense of permanency, of *rootedness*, for which we feel gratitude. Go back over your list and remind yourself of how much these things mean to you and how thankful you truly are for them. Did you list family? Music? The beauty of nature? Friends? The loving presence of God, if you're spiritually inclined? Are there more things you can add to your list?

Notice the wording under the column marked "Change." It doesn't say "Things that stink in my life" or "That awful force that throws everything out of control." It says only "Things I wish were different." This is an important perspective shift. Under this column, we can list things we see in our lives that need to be different from the way they are at this moment. Such a list is not judgmental; we're not assigning a negative connotation to these things, simply making ourselves aware that we know what we want to be different.

Now we can review both columns. Don't be alarmed if you have more items listed under "Change" than under "Constants." Each of our constants carries much more weight than any individual element of change.

It is important to view constants and change as parts of the same system rather than in isolation. As long as we understand and work *with* them, they will work in conjunction, synergistically, for our greater good. Change is course correction and a product of the physical world in which all things change. It allows us to better appreciate the eternal values and constants that enrich our lives. Constants, those things we love and know, are always with us and *produce no stress* (see Figure 1.5). Quite the opposite in fact: they comfort us and help us feel at peace and secure. Change, on the other hand, can produce high levels of stress, especially when we don't understand it and feel that it threatens our self-control.

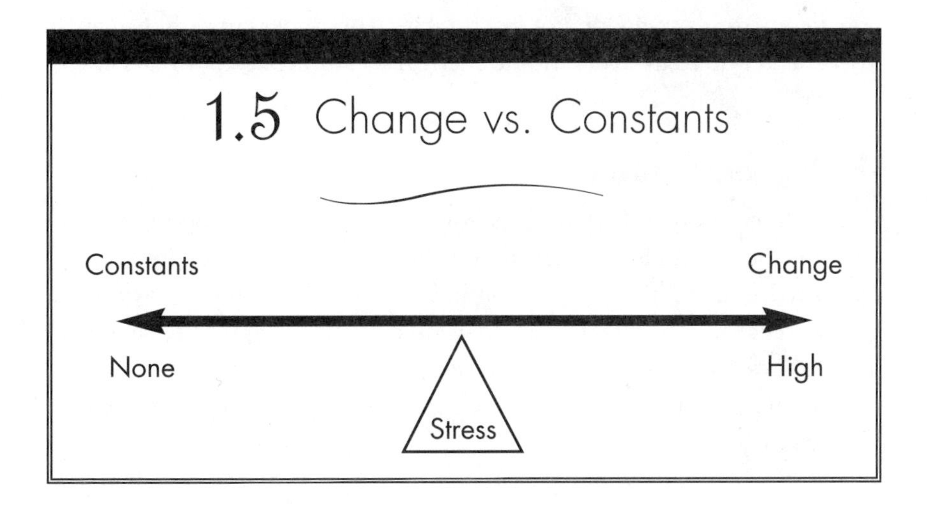

Cursed or Blessed?

If you add their ages together, the authors of this little book have been on this earth for an entire century. In that time they've had a wealth of experiences, all of which can be interpreted quite differently depending on how we view them.

A few of the more pivotal collective events:

- Abandoned by father at birth.
- Abandoned by mother at age four.
- Removed from abusive family and sent to orphanage at age four.
- Used as human ashtray by foster family father.
- Adopted and unadopted (returned to orphanage) twice before age seven.

- Sent to Vietnam.
- Entered into an arranged marriage.
- Had "special" child.
- Lost spouse to medical malpractice.

Any of these events could be seen as seriously challenging, to say the least. And we definitely struggled with them; understand that we can talk about stress and its aftermath very intimately. In addition to these personal challenges, we have both experienced professional lives replete with the usual misfortunes, plus some truly bizarre happenstances. Were these experiences curses or blessings? We cannot casually reframe any of these horrific events as some kind of inscrutable benefit, of course. But in *every* instance, it's up to us to determine the real meaning of each situation and its significance in our lives.

The Bigger Picture

Our lives and our work are a constant interplay between the Big Picture and the gritty details of everyday routine. It's certainly possible to live only in the immediacy of physical activity, making a buck, paying the bills, and getting through the day, day after day after day. Many people do live this way. But it is the sense of purpose, the quest for meaning, the coming in contact with the numinous and applying it to the particulars of our everyday lives that create lasting joy and fulfillment. As educators, we want to make the world better by helping students learn far more than the content of their curricula. We relish dealing with both the philosophical issues and their practical applications.

Years ago, Lou found a very useful way to shift his focus off immediate pressures and onto the Big Picture. Making this shift is immensely helpful in keeping a balanced perspective. In Figure 1.6 we present an adaptation of his exercise as a way to add depth and meaning to daily living.

The morning after you conduct the exercise in Figure 1.6, take a few moments to reconnect with the pulse of the parking lot. Think of the talents, skills, and resources you can bring into play to change those lives for the better. Be thankful for the opportunity to make a difference.

1.6 The School Parking Lot

The next time you have 20 minutes or half an hour free at the end of the day, sit where you can view the school parking lot and watch the students closely as they leave. Try to imagine what might be going on in their lives at this moment. What can you surmise from the kinds of cars that students or their parents drive, from their interactions with parents or peers, from their body language as they anticipate the rest of their day? Give full reign to your imagination:

- Look at that old Chrysler with the fender missing that's spewing black fumes out the exhaust pipe. It has a presidential campaign bumper sticker on it. Does the candidate choice seem incongruous with the condition of the car? Why might that be?
- Spot the shiny red Camaro with flashy magnesium wheels. What kind of deals financed that automobile purchase? What is the driver saying to the students who just walked up to look at the car? What is he handing the students?
- Notice the elderly woman standing beside her aging Volvo with an anxious look on her face. She seems to be looking for someone. Is it her grandson? Where are the parents? Are they working and too busy for the child?
- Check out the pickup truck with a new lawnmower in the back. Does the driver do landscaping, or is this machine to mow the lawn of the family's new home?

Continue this exercise, car after car, person after person, until the last car has left the parking lot. Store the images and the imaginary stories in your heart. Think of the meaning behind this slice of the mercurial flow of life.

2

The Work Ethic

I'm very happy to announce that Bob in human resources is this week's winner of our prestigious Red Badge of Courage. The citation on his award inspires us all: "Bob is a model employee. He puts in a solid 40-hour workweek—every two days." Bob set a bold new standard for the Red Badge last week when he had a heart attack right in the middle of his PowerPoint presentation to the Board. As he collapsed to the floor, still clutching the laser pointer, he barked bravely, "Next slide."

You'll be pleased to know that Bob is in stable condition and should be back to work this week. He sends his thanks for the Red Badge and the bevy of accompanying prizes. He particularly appreciated the two-quart coffee mug and the laminated reference card inscribed with the names of his children.

The Red Badge of Courage

Just as society confers Purple Hearts on its wounded soldiers, it gives, at least metaphorically, the Red Badge to brave souls like Bob, who work tirelessly with no concern for their own personal safety or well-being. Certainly there is nothing wrong with hard work, but somewhere along the line, the concept of diligent labor has become distorted.

As best we can tell, the Pilgrims were the ones who first started shifting the meaning of hard work. After all, consider the life expectancy of the average Pilgrim: before even reaching today's legal drinking age, many were devoured by wild animals or died from cold, starvation, or giving birth. So how did they cope? How did they enjoy life during their short time on Earth? They seized the day and announced, "Let's eat, drink, and be merry; for tomorrow, we die." No, wait—that was the Epicureans; the Pilgrims are the ones who masterminded the Protestant work ethic. By handpicking scriptural passages and taking them out of context, they built a credible case for a workaholic existence so dour that most colonists anticipated their first experience with joy would come only in the afterlife.

No one does anything without expecting some kind of a payoff, and several aspects of overwork can make it seem worthwhile. Granted, some organizational cultures expect or even demand overwork. Many people feel that time spent on work directly reflects their personal value; others simply believe that their work cannot be done in less time than they devote to it, though this is rarely true. The payoff of overwork is often defensive, as it can provide us with cover from personal issues that we would just as soon not have to handle. (See Figure 2.1 to assess the effect of your work on your personal life.)

2.1 Pause and Apply

If you routinely work more than 50 hours a week, you may be an overworker. Take a moment and consider whether there are any hidden reasons that you work so much. Is it just a familiar and therefore comfortable pattern? Make a list of what you might do with the extra time if you weren't working such long hours:

____

____

____

If nothing in particular comes to mind, there's a good chance that your "work" has acquired an importance beyond the actual tasks at hand. If you can think of many things you'd rather do with your time, then you recognize that you're working too much.

Death by Overwork

But surely working too hard won't kill us, right? Wrong. Health activists in Japan now claim they lose over 30,000 workers a year to *karoshi*—death by overwork.[1]

Strictly speaking, it isn't the *work* but the *stressful reaction to work* that affects so many people. A few statistics reveal the pervasiveness and the severity of the problem:

- Seventy to 90 percent of all doctor visits in the United States today are for stress-related disorders.[2]
- Americans consume 5 billion tranquilizers, 5 billion barbiturates, 3 billion amphetamines, and 16,000 tons of aspirin every year in an effort to cope with stress.[3]
- In a 10-year study, people who were unable to manage their stress effectively had a 40 percent higher death rate than nonstressed individuals.[4]
- A 20-year study conducted by the University of London School of Medicine has shown that unmanaged stress is a more dangerous risk factor for cancer and heart disease than cigarette smoking or eating high-cholesterol foods.[5]
- According to a Mayo Clinic study of people with heart disease, psychological stress is the strongest predictor of future cardiac events, including cardiac death, cardiac arrest, and heart attack.[6]

The Physiological Reaction

What happens, physiologically, when we broadcast a stress alert? Our body launches more than 1,400 known physical and chemical reactions and over 30 hormones and neurotransmitters. The two primary branches of the autonomic nervous system (ANS) are the first to react.[7] Though it's something of an oversimplification, it's commonly said that the *sympathetic* branch of the ANS handles the "fight or flight" response to stress. By contrast the *parasympathetic* branch directs the "rest and digest" functions.[8] In general, the sympathetic branch is responsible for expending energy, while the parasympathetic branch is responsible for energy conservation and restoration. Both branches work together to balance our body's systems, a process called homeostasis.[9]

The problem arises when negative reaction to stressors becomes chronic and the parasympathetic nervous system doesn't have time to help us recover because the sympathetic nervous system is always activated. A little wine is good for the heart, but nonstop whine is another matter. Once the "stress hormones"—adrenaline, noradrenaline, and cortisol—

begin flowing in a steady stream, they "sear the body like a constant drizzle of acid."[10]

Stress, Memory, and High-Stakes Testing

According to the National Institutes of Health, high levels of cortisol are particularly harmful to the hippocampus—a region of the brain that is involved with spatial and verbal memory.[11] Researchers at McGill University have found that the hippocampi of older people with high levels of cortisol are 14 percent smaller than those of people with moderate cortisol levels.[12]

Another study at the University of Zurich in Switzerland and the University of California, Irvine tested 18 men and 18 women between the ages of 20 and 40. The subjects were given lists to memorize and were tested on their recall before and after taking cortisone tablets (which the body processes into cortisol). Not surprisingly, recall was found to be impaired following ingestion of the tablets. The researchers concluded that high cortisol levels "may induce retrieval impairments in such stressful situations as examinations, job interviews, combat, and courtroom testimony."[13] "Retrieval impairments"? Now there's a term that could replace "test anxiety" in the Dictionary of Educationalese! The *San Jose Mercury News* reported that in California, where state sanctions are scheduled to kick in for schools that have failed to improve their scores on standardized tests, stress levels are at an all-time high for staff as well as students. The state sanctions can include displacing the staff, or even state takeover of the school. With only 60 percent of elementary and 29 percent of high schools hitting their targets, State Superintendent Delaine Eastin said, "Hopefully people are waking up and understanding this is for real."[14]

Call us incredulous, but we don't have much faith that this chronic cortisol approach to accountability can do anything to improve schools. In fact, it reminds us of debtor's prison, an institution the French had the wisdom to abolish in 1789. *Allons, enfants*—we can do better than this.

Life's Little Stresses

As Russian playwright Anton Chekhov put it most pithily, "Any idiot can handle a crisis. It's day-to-day living that wears you out." Who wants to return home from a conference to face 438 e-mail messages, or a mailbox full of junk mail? And how many advertisements do you think the average American sees each day, including labels and logos? According to Dharma Singh Khalsa:

> The answer is 16,000.[15] Each ad, of course, does not send us into a screaming panic—but it *does* register upon our brain's nervous system, taxing our brain cells and neurotransmitters, and sometimes causing release of stress hormones. And these are just *ads*—not news messages, radio programs, Muzak, job-related information, movies, books, or magazines.

Strangely, our minds often manufacture stress reactions from thin air. Our subconscious mind, where the autonomic nervous system responses are generated, doesn't know or care where the reaction came from; it will generate "appropriate" responses even if the source of the so-called stress is really "upstairs" in the brain.

Consider the driver who cuts you off in traffic. If you react in anger, you've assigned a motivation to the driver—rudeness, for example—that may not actually exist; for all you know, the driver never saw you and wasn't even aware that he'd cut you off. This impression, therefore, arises from your own injured ego, and your body reacts by dutifully dumping cortisol and adrenaline throughout your body. The driver goes blissfully on his way while you pay the price for your perception of his motivation. By deciding to interpret the event as a personal affront, you automatically add real physical injury to an invented psychological insult. Doc Childre and Howard Martin describe the pattern: "When things stifle or annoy us, we all have our favorite ways of reacting. Some people immediately lash out in anger, while others use caustic humor to get some sense of compensation. Some turn to drinking, drugs, or binge eating to stave off feelings of frustration or entrapment. And almost all of us complain on a regular basis—whenever we get together with our friends."[16] Unfortunately, these complaining sessions drain our strength "like an emotional virus" and reinforce "a damaging neural habit in our brains, making it easier for us to feel miserable the next time."[17]

To find out how often we invoke the anger response instead of the care response in a typical day, try recording your own emotional reactions to situations, events, and people in your life in the tally sheet in Figure 2.2. If you feel other emotions that aren't listed here, go ahead and add those words to the appropriate column. If you want to jot down the times, that's okay too—whatever gives you the most accurate picture of your emotional day.

2.2 Pause and Apply

Red Badge of Courage	Sweet Balm of Calm
anger, anxiety, confusion, depression, disappointment, fear, frustration, guilt, hopelessness, impatience, irritation, regret, resentment, sarcasm, worry…	appreciation, clarity, compassion, empathy, faith, gentleness, goodness, gratitude, happiness, hope, humor, joy, kindness, love, patience, peace, thankfulness, warmth…
Example: 6:00 a.m. "Oh @#(&*, it's morning." (anger, frustration)	*Example:* 6:00 a.m. "Oh, what a beautiful morning!" (appreciation, hope, joy)
Total entries =	Total entries =

Every entry in the left column is another blow to your health and well-being. All negative emotional states—resentment, anger, frustration, worry, disappointment—take a toll on your heart, your brain, and the rest of your body.[18]

Researchers at the Institute of HeartMath conducted a study to demonstrate the effects of positive and negative emotions on the immune system. When participants in the study spent five minutes just *recalling* the *feeling* of anger, they experienced a short-term rise in IgA (an immune system antibody) followed by depletion so severe that it took the immune system over six hours to recover. Recalling the feeling of care and compassion, on the other hand, spiked IgA levels by an average of 34 percent, followed by a return to baseline, then gentle climbing above baseline throughout the next six hours.[19]

James Wilson points out in his book *Adrenal Fatigue: The 21st-Century Stress Syndrome*, our hurried lifestyle "leaves little room for an adequate adrenal response when the adrenal glands never get the chance to recoup and are already responding at their maximum capacity.

"The more we understand about the physiology of stress," Wilson continues, "the more obvious it is that unless we quickly evolve to have adrenal glands the size of footballs, we must learn to give our adrenals the opportunity they need to recover on a regular basis. Otherwise, we will rapidly devolve into a society of the chronically sick and tired that even coffee, colas, and other stimulants cannot rally."[20]

The Overachiever's Point of View

How we perceive a person, place, or event determines whether our body goes into the stress-alert mode. If we think the situation is too demanding, our body believes us; if we sense that we have too few options, our reaction to stress blinds us to the resources we actually have available to us.

Some personality types are more prone to stress than others. For example, "Type A" individuals seem to thrive on stress. They get "hooked" on the feelings of confidence and elation associated with the release of noradrenalin and actually seek out high-stress situations. As they indulge more and more in stress-inducing behavior, they eventually become addicted to the "rush" that accompanies it.[21]

Although quieter and less obviously hyperactive than Type A individuals, overachievers are just as much at risk from stress-related illnesses.

"Dependable, cheerful, and seemingly always able to cope, they refuse to give in to illness or fatigue and cannot refuse excessive demands made on them," writes Alix Kirsta in *The Book of Stress Survival.* "Perfectionists by nature, they are often driven by fear of falling short of their own expectations of themselves. They also tend to place the needs of others before their own and can find it hard to express their deepest feelings."[22]

Working mothers often fall into the overachieving, overcaring trap. For believers, service to the church can bring overwhelming demands. (One can never do too much for God!) But as Liz Curtis Higgs reminds us in her hilariously practical book, *Only Angels Can Wing It*, even God rested on Sunday.[23]

Like ducks seeming to glide serenely on the lake while paddling like mad underwater, many of us make the "I-can-do-it-all" approach to life look easy—while putting in twenty-hour days to pull it off. Workaholism and its twin, perfectionism, are increasing problems in our society. When will we realize that we don't need to be the best at everything? As Barbara Billingsley (the mom on *Leave It To Beaver*) confessed, "Even June Cleaver didn't keep her house in perfect order—the prop man did it."[24] We just need to do what we do well and get help with the rest.

As we spend more and more time at work and less and less time doing anything else, we risk becoming synonymous with what we do for a living. (We identify with the webbed feet under the water rather than with the beautiful duck above.) As for the Red Badge of Courage: hang enough of those around the duck's neck, and no amount of caffeine will be able to keep him afloat.

If you start to take yourself too seriously, if your paddling becomes frenetic, or if the truths in this chapter hit a little too close to home, take a moment to imagine yourself floating on the local duck pond. If no one is within earshot, try quacking a few times. (Quackery: that's our best medical advice.)

3

It's About Time

Next time you find yourself in a long line at the grocery store, ask the people behind you if they have a minute to help with a survey you are conducting. Would they be so kind as to share their top 10 "peeves" about daily life? (Since they are stuck in line anyway, they will probably take the time to respond.) Based on our own extensive surveys of this nature, we can comfortably predict that 9 of their 10 complaints will relate to time. Regardless of their profession, "not enough time" will surpass "not enough money" as the single biggest complaint.

Life After Teaching

For teachers, time pressures can be particularly daunting. The Hamilton Trust, an independent educational charity based in Oxford, England, has found that 54-hour workweeks are the norm for teachers in that country. The study concluded that long hours may explain why about half of all teachers leave the field within four years of entering it; as teacher Caroline Hall says, "I'll keep going as long as I can, but there's no way I could imagine being a teacher if I had a family."[1]

In an effort to stave off the exodus of teachers, the Trust has recently posted math and literacy lesson plans on its Web site to help reduce the amount of preparation time teachers spend at home. Between December 27, 2001, and January 9, 2002, more than 33,000 documents were downloaded from the site. A sad commentary on teacher desperation (or a measure of how little life they have left outside of work), the site even recorded significant traffic on Christmas Day![2]

Picking Up the Pace

From the Sunday stroll to the Saturday power walk, from "whenever it's convenient" to "I need it yesterday," from the horsewhip to the accelerator pedal, the 20th century was less like a hundred-years-passed and more like a hundred-yard dash. Even our speech patterns started to capture the clip: the United States federal government became "the feds," the Internal Revenue Service became the IRS—even Federal Express was reduced to FedEx. "Those extra syllables, it seems, took too long to say."[3]

Journalist Ted Anthony shares a few other milestones from the harried, hurried century ("pared down, of course, to keep this quick").

In transportation:

- 1903: the first speed limit (England, 20 MPH)
- 1908: the Ford Model T (top speed: 45 MPH)
- 1933: the Boeing 247 (150 MPH)
- 1968: Apollo 8's astronauts (24,791 MPH)

In information processing:

- 1922: *Reader's Digest* was founded to give busy people abridged versions of articles they wouldn't otherwise have time to read.
- 1965: Moore's Law proclaimed that data processing speed doubles every 18 months.
- As we speak: labs in New Mexico, California, and New York are competing to build a computer that performs more than 1 trillion calculations per second (the equivalent of every person on Earth doing 200 sums on a pocket calculator in one second).[4]

In the middle of the 20th century, you couldn't turn around without hearing somebody extol the wonders that technology would bring in the coming 50 years. Surely in that distant Golden Age of 2000, labor as we knew it would be a thing of the past as fabulous machines would do much of our work, thus affording mankind the leisure to pursue its loftiest endeavors. Disease, hunger, war, and oppression of any kind would come to an end because we could free up our intellects to achieve more noble goals.

Perhaps you missed the news, but the year 2000 came and went. We are now officially in that glorious age of saved time. No doubt you lost track of this development because you were off terrascaping Mars for imminent colonization now that, thanks to the magic of technology, you no longer have to pick up the kids, grade papers manually, program your VCR, juggle conflicting appointments, or feel otherwise overloaded.

The crystal ball through which everything once seemed so clear is now just so much broken glass. People complain more today about the lack of leisure time than they did at any point in the last century. What no one saw coming was how the pace of our lives would pick up to match the speed of work, now turbocharged through technology. Even animals have learned to accommodate themselves to the pulse of technology, as one writer to *Reader's Digest* indicated. When she logged onto AOL and that little voice announced "you've got mail," her dogs would settle down and get comfortable; as soon as they heard the voice say "good-bye," they jumped up and went to the door, ready for a walk.[5]

We acclimate all too easily to more speed, falling prey to the illusion that it's somehow better. A few years ago when our friend David Thornburg went off for a two-week conference, he invited his office manager, a delightful lady in her 70s, to use his computer in his absence. When he returned, she went back to her old machine, and shortly thereafter complained to him that there was something wrong with it. "It's slowed down," she said.

Have we become empowered by technology or enslaved to it? As authors David Mahoney and Richard Restak suggest in *The Longevity Strategy*:

> Unless you're a doctor or someone likely to become involved in life-or-death situations, do you really need a pager, a cell phone, and a laptop computer during your weekend at the beach? Granted, many of these technological information gatherers and dispensers serve the purpose of ego massage. But such perks can carry a higher price than simply their cost. Impatience, the feeling of being chronically overloaded, jitteriness, burnout, overindulgence in alcohol—these are some of the costs exacted if you don't control information technology rather than letting it control you.[6]

For just one day, try to live your life without electricity (batteries included). Think twice about any devices you could or would not do without.

Two for One

We humans have done some extraordinary things in our quest to harness time: from TV dinners to bathroom reading, we're always trying to multitask. Lynell, for example, once asked her father for an extension cord when she was a teenager. "I thought I could save time by drying my hair while I was in the bathtub," she explained.

Teachers are the masters of the two-for-one use of time (see Figure 3.1). Assigned to supervise after-school detention? Take that time to make calls home to parents with good news about their children. If the parents aren't home, leave a message. Give specific praise for the child, such as "Make sure to ask Johnny about his presentation on the American Indians—his research on war paint and those full-color slides for the PowerPoint were awesome!" or "Just wanted to let you know how moved I was by Suzie's kindness this morning. The letter she wrote to the school in Afghanistan revealed a tender and loving heart. You are clearly doing an excellent job of teaching her values. I hope you're planning to have more children—at least as long as I'm at this school!" One 4th grade teacher who made these kinds of calls without changing anything else about her teaching was voted teacher of the year by the parents, who clearly appreciated the communication.

3.1 Pause and Apply

- Make a list of ways you do two things at once in your professional and personal life.
- Ask friends/colleagues to do the same.
- Share your lists to see what you can learn from one another.

To Do or Not to Do

Educators spend valuable time reading books about and attending workshops on time management. Energized and motivated, we follow the latest system to prioritize this and color code that. Sometimes the ideas help, because we can stick with most things, at least for a while: hence the plethora of plans that promise to help you lose weight or get organized in a specified number of weeks, days, hours, or even minutes. The "One-

Minute" promises are, of course, the most seductive: one minute for rice, slimmer hips, more loving relationships, etc.

By the time we organize, categorize, and prioritize everything, it seems as if we have no time left to work. We agree that for many people, it's helpful to make a "To-Do" list from time to time; prioritizing tasks is probably a good way to make sure we don't forget critically important items. We actually found a little notepad that works splendidly for that purpose. It invites you to place your tasks for the day under one of four categories: to do, will do, must do, and deep do.

The "deep do" reminds us of the cartoon of a baby's backside, captioned "I'm a little behind!" These days, most of us are more than a little behind. In an article entitled "Don't Manage Time, Manage Yourself," David Beardsley states that the average person has a chronic backlog of 200 to 300 hours of uncompleted work—which puts each one of us approximately one month behind![7]

How do we live with this kind of pressure? According to humorist Scott Friedman, by reframing the way we think about our "To-Do" lists. Instead of just automatically adding every project, goal, and opportunity that comes our way to our lists, we must become "connoisseurs of *possible* to-dos." Rather than an endless litany of obligations, to-do lists should reflect our passions and priorities. Make it an honor to get on the list.[8] Instead of being ruled by the tyranny of the urgent, we should let our lives be regulated by what Lynell refers to as our "Coeur Values" (*coeur* being French for "heart"). A visual representation of how we spend our time can help illustrate whether we are actually following these values. The commonsense, four-quadrants time-analysis chart developed by Time/Design (Figure 3.2) is as profound as it is simple.

When life feels as if it's spinning out of control, it's usually because we are spending too much time on tasks that are Urgent (to others) but not especially Important (to us). To break this cycle, we need to take a look each day at items on our list that are neither important nor urgent and decide *quickly* which tasks can be delegated or relegated *before* they become emergencies. Next—and this is where the payoff comes in—we need to spend a minimum of one hour every day in the Important/Not Urgent quadrant. This time should be sacred. In many jobs, we need to reserve this time at the beginning or the end of the day—before or after anyone else is around.

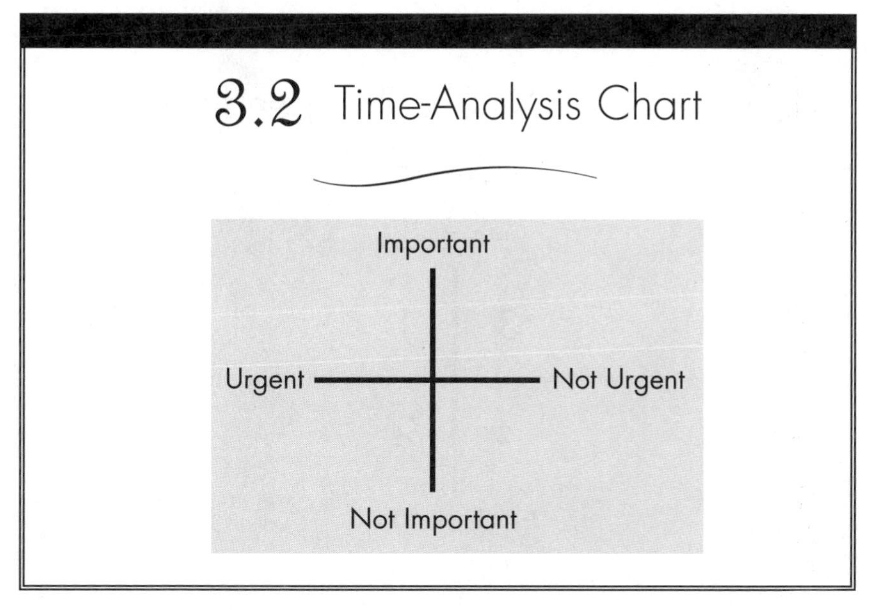

We run into trouble when life in the other quadrants has us so exhausted that we can't muster the energy to spend that extra hour. Yet it is only in that precious time that we can research and ponder those things that are most important for our professional and personal lives. (Consider using Figures 3.3 and 3.4 to diagram and evaluate your own daily activities.)

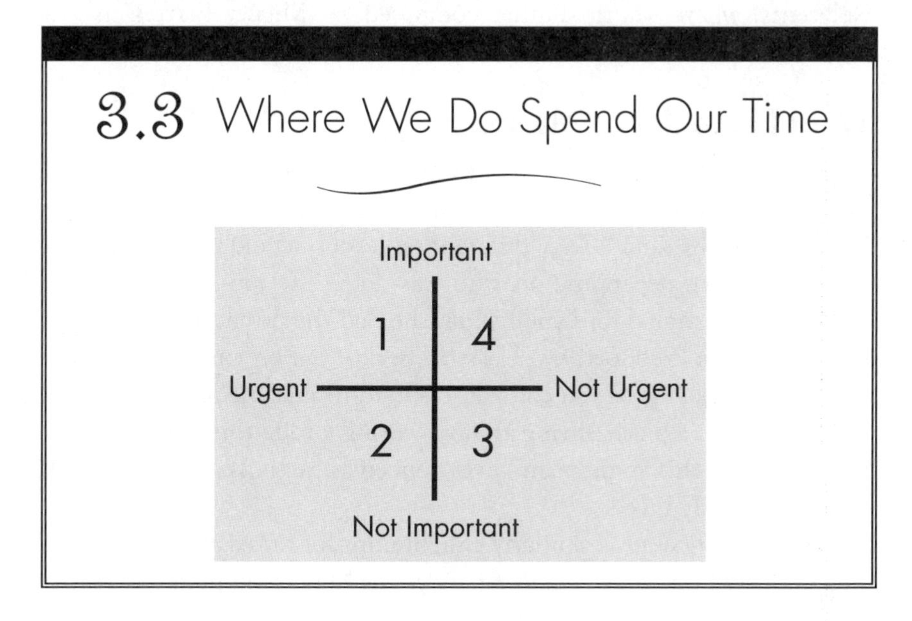

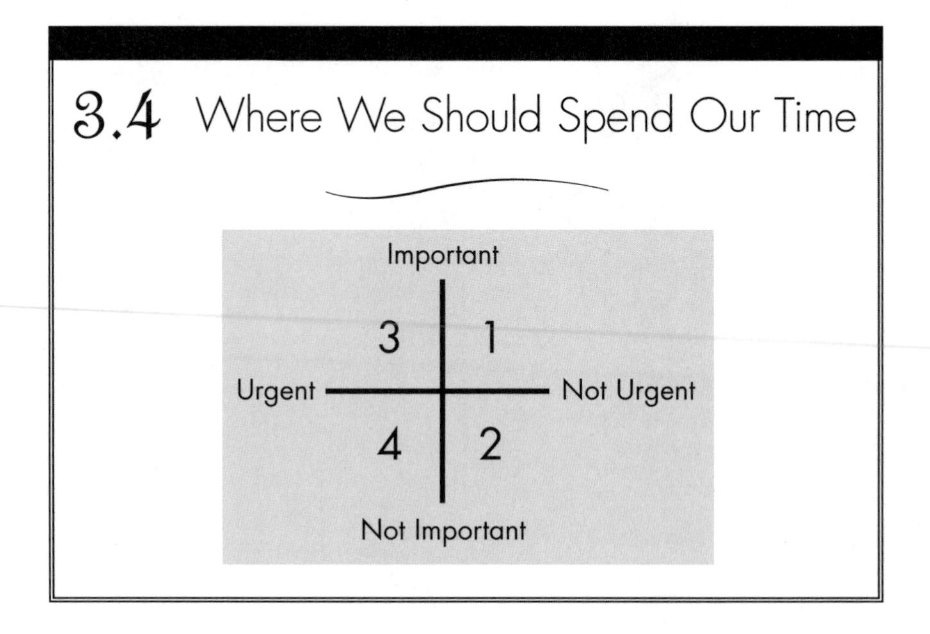

Because we are not stressed out working in the Important/Not Urgent quadrant, all our neurons are freed up to do their best thinking. The creative juices can flow, the "right brain" can frolic, and the imagination can soar. This is the quadrant where Einstein discovered the Theory of Relativity, where Martin Luther composed "A Mighty Fortress Is Our God," where Paul McCartney found the melody to "Yesterday."

What I Love About My Job

In looking at the four-quadrant model, it occurred to us that the same tasks could fall into different quadrants depending on who was creating the chart. By the same token, different professions could be seen as stressful or enjoyable depending on who was doing the job. This point was beautifully illustrated for Lynell when she had the privilege of meeting a firefighter from Prudhoe Bay, Alaska. Check it out on a map; it's as close to Santa's workshop as you can get. It's hard to imagine anyone wanting to work in such a place, sitting around waiting for life-threatening fires to break out. Yet this young man's eyes danced as he spoke about his work, which he clearly loved.

Another encounter, similarly enlightening, occurred after a workshop we conducted on career planning. A young lady came up afterwards to discuss career choices. She was completing an M.A. in education at Harvard and planned to become a teacher, but her friends were telling her that this would be a serious waste of all the time and money she had spent on her education. She wondered if maybe she shouldn't pursue a career as a school principal instead—at least the pay would be better. Lynell suggested that she try "shadowing" a principal for a day to see what the job was like because, from Lynell's observations, principals have a very tough job, facing emergencies and crises nonstop throughout the day—much like medical triage in a trauma center or on the battlefield.

At that point, a lady still seated in the front row blurted out, "That's what I *love* about the job! I'm very good at making those quick decisions, and I feel like I've really accomplished something when the day is over." It turns out that the lady principal was also the young lady's mother. They decided to take Lynell's advice and have the daughter follow her mother around for a day to see if she could picture herself in that kind of role.

Clearly, the *person* has more influence than the *job description* in determining the pressures of any particular profession. An article in *Ladies Home Journal* magazine compared the stress levels of people in four very different jobs: a business executive, an intensive care nurse, a stay-at-home mom, and a hairdresser. On the surface, one would expect the first three to be the most stressed. Yet of the four women interviewed, it was the hairdresser who experienced the highest level of stress. Why? She could not make herself get up early enough to avoid a frantic race to work every morning! The self-created time pressure caused more stress for the hairdresser than the obvious challenges did for either of the other three women![9]

To Everything There Is a Season

The children had all been photographed, and the teacher was trying to persuade them each to buy a copy of the group photograph.

"Just think how nice it will be to look at it when you are all grown up and say: 'There's Jennifer. She's a lawyer,' or 'That's Michael. He's a doctor.'"

A small voice at the back of the room rang out, "And there's the teacher. She's dead."

Generations come and go. Too often, it seems illogical (to say nothing of unjust and sad) when people who have touched our lives are taken from us. In most cases, though, we concede that nature has the rhythm right. As we celebrate the changing of the seasons, we feel a certain calm reassurance, like the beating of a healthy heart. People, on the other hand, often seem to move to the speed of some truly erratic drummers.

In his foreword to *The HeartMath Solution*, Stephan Rechtschaffen writes: "Most of us in modern society feel that we never have enough time—a feeling that results in the frenzy and hurry that underlie all our stress and lead to serious diseases and disorders. Recognizing that time is the rhythmic dimension of life, I've begun to see that health is a delicate balance of rhythm, while dis-ease results from dis-rhythm."[10]

There are cycles in every aspect of our lives. The human body itself vibrates at a rate that represents its own native pace of 0.1 cycles per second. This is called its *resonant frequency*. All things, both living and inanimate, have their own resonant frequencies. When we are aligned with cycles, we've literally "got it together"—an expression which itself reflects our innate synchronization with the natural rhythms of life.

In the 1960s, "Turn Turn Turn," a song by Pete Seeger that became a huge hit by The Byrds, reminded us of Solomon's Old Testament musings on the flow of life: "To everything there is a season and a time for every purpose under heaven"—

> A time to be born, and a time to die;
> A time to plant, and a time to pluck what is planted;
> A time to kill, and a time to heal;
> A time to break down, and a time to build up;
> A time to weep, and a time to laugh;
> A time to mourn, and a time to dance;
> A time to cast away stones, and a time to gather stones;
> A time to embrace, and a time to refrain from embracing;
> A time to gain, and a time to lose;
> A time to keep, and a time to throw away;
> A time to tear, and a time to sew;
> A time to keep silence, and a time to speak;
> A time to love, and a time to hate;
> A time of war, and a time of peace.
>
> — Ecclesiastes 3:1–8

Like swimming against the tide, fighting these cycles can only exhaust us. We're far better off seeing how we might work *with* the cycles rather than *against* them. Some cycles are as plain as night and day, such as our circadian (daily) rhythms. The brain's timekeeper needs the 24-hour cycle of light and dark to set itself properly. Although individuals reach their peak and function better at different times during the day (some of us are "early birds," some are "night owls," some are still wondering when we're going to wake up), the patterns in Figure 3.5 apply to most people.[11]

3.5 Circadian Rhythm Patterns

Time of Day	Physical and Mental State
7–9 a.m.	Mental fog but best time to burn calories.
9 a.m.–noon	Levels of stress hormones such as cortisol peak; analytical skill and mental performance are increased.
Noon–2 p.m.	Alertness and verbal reasoning peak.
3 p.m.–7 p.m.	Long-term memory peaks, and alertness rises.
7–9 p.m.	Thinking skills wind down.

These patterns help explain why we have so little success asking teenagers to do math from 7:30 to 8:30 a.m., English from 2:00 to 3:00 p.m., and homework between 7:00 and 9:00 p.m. This may also explain why many teachers drink coffee from buckets.

Twenty-five million Americans put in over ten hours a day at the office.[12] Are those long hours at the school or the office really productive? We can't make the day longer or the night shorter; we can, however, understand our circadian cycles and work with them. We can put the right task at the right time of day, including a time for rest. A lifestyle without rest produces a restless life.

Time and Tide Wait for No One

Funny how time creeps by glacially when we're having an unpleasant experience, yet slips away imperceptibly when we're enjoying ourselves. Surely it ought to be the other way around. But however we experience time, we are virtually unanimous in desiring more of it. When Einstein's Theory of Relativity revealed that time moves slower (albeit by scant split seconds) at higher altitudes, some people actually moved to the mountains in an effort to prolong their lives.

4

Throw Your Clutter in the Gutter

In a memorable episode of the television show "The West Wing," fictional U.S. president Josiah Bartlett talks to his psychiatrist about his four-day bout with insomnia. When the analyst asks if he is experiencing any stress in his job, the president replies with a short laundry list of his current political challenges and concludes, "No more than usual." Then he adds, "I don't like the word 'stress.' It's a Madison Avenue term. It's something you can fix with flavored coffee and bath bubbles."

We can only fantasize about the annual revenue of companies that produce bath bubbles in this country. Personally, we'd rather take showers: you can multitask (try washing your hair in the bathtub!); it's easier to wipe down the shower than scrub the tub; and most important, the acoustics are better for singing in the shower. Bath or shower? Is one better than the other? Yes: whichever works for you.

Seriously, what *can* help relieve the feeling of stress? We have read most of the stress-busting books and magazines published in the last 30 years. We have listened to the tapes, watched the videos, gone to the lectures, and interviewed the experts. Many of the speeches, writings, and products contain information and strategies that we have found useful to varying degrees. Generally they fall in the broad category of stress management. Although we hold that stress is not something to be managed—a point we will expound on in Chapter 9—we concede that certain aspects of the "bubble-bath approach" could be useful and, in some cases, even fun. In the next few chapters, we will share what we consider to be the best of these ideas, beginning with reclaiming space.

The Curse of Kadema

For the record, Lou does not now nor has he ever had a problem with clutter. Lynell has watched him with a garbage bag. The man is relentless. "Haven't used this in the last 15 minutes? It's history!"

Lynell, on the other hand, stores her junk mail in her nonfunctioning oven. A neighbor recommended a housekeeper named Kadema who was guaranteed to leave the place spotless. This sounded like a wonderful idea until it became apparent that Lynell would have to spend six to eight hours every other Friday clearing the clutter so that Kadema could find the floors and counters when she came to clean every other Saturday. Soon, the bimonthly clutter-clearing routine became so irritating that Lynell dubbed it "the curse of Kadema."

Lou—who soon learned that Fridays were not good days to suggest collaborative work sessions and Saturday mornings were definitely not a good time to call for any reason—finally ventured to suggest that there might be a way to reframe Kadema's visits. Lynell gave Lou's suggestion—to deal with clutter proactively—serious consideration. Thanks to Lou, Lynell began to reclaim her house, counter by counter, room by room, so that Fridays could be freed up for more meaningful pursuits. She began to enjoy the way the house felt after Kadema worked her magic, like a gentle rain that leaves the air fresh and full of promise. Lynell now looks forward to this bimonthly blessing, which she gratefully refers to as the "*kiss* of Kadema."

How the Stars Deal with Clutter

Movies and television would have us believe that there are two types of people with respect to clutter. Remember "The Odd Couple"? Felix Unger was a compulsive neatnik, and his roommate Oscar Madison gave new dimension to the term "sloppy." At some level, they both had their admirable qualities. Felix tended to excel at everything, and Oscar had a puppy-dog quality that made him irresistibly lovable. Looking back, however, it is apparent that neither Felix nor Oscar made a very good role model. Yes, Felix had everything in order, but his fastidiousness was driven by a very unhealthy personality—a heart full of "shoulds" and "musts" and a mind weighed down with obligations. As for Oscar, his trail of cookie and potato chip crumbs marked the confused path of a man with no clear direction in life. How could he clean his room when his life was a mess?

Certainly it is a gross oversimplification to say that a cluttered home, office, or classroom represents a confused mind, any more than it is to say that an empty area reflects some kind of inner vacuum. Yet to some degree, we clutterholics might want to consider that the clutter could reflect a life with too many priorities and too little space into which to stuff them.

The Chinese Perspective: Feng Shui

Followers of Feng Shui will tell you that there is an ongoing dialogue between your inner thoughts and feelings and the physical space you create around yourself. When Patricia, a Feng Shui consultant, visited Lynell's home, she suggested starting with the spaces that would attract the eye upon entering each room and using that space to make a positive statement about the purpose of the room. For instance, Patricia explained that items on the counter of the bay window in Lynell's master bedroom should be arranged in pairs, to signify the welcoming of a love relationship: two vases of flowers, two candles, two semiprecious stones. She was not enthusiastic about Lynell's suggestion of two piles of laundry, which unfortunately made up the decor on the day of her visit.

In Lynell's dining room, the dominant piece of furniture is an elegant glass-doored china cabinet—the perfect place to display items that speak of beauty, love of family, and the value of family gatherings. Prominently displayed, they help nurture the spirit as well as the body.

Once you dedicate the most eye-catching place in a room to a highest purpose, it becomes much easier to reorganize it. Patricia recommends that you continue to face this part of the room while cleaning, working your way back toward the entry door. A visible reminder of purpose makes it easier to decide what should remain and what should be moved elsewhere, recycled, or discarded. To get a sense of how Feng Shui principles might apply to your home or school, try the exercise in Figure 4.1.

4.1 Pause and Apply

Take a moment to inventory the "entry view" of the rooms in your life: rooms in your home, your office, and your classroom.

- What is the first thing you see when you walk in the door?
- What does that say about what is important to you?
- What emotions and attitudes do the items on display reveal and communicate to others?

Tips from the Queen of Clutter

As the former and now reformed Queen of Clutter, Lynell would like to share some insights she picked up during her many trips to the dumpster. First, imagine your work or living space with a river flowing through it, from the entrance to the exit. Whenever something comes in the front door, something else must go out the back; otherwise, the flow is blocked, and the place becomes stagnant. A good day is when you can bring *one* thing in and move *three* things out. Let's say you buy a pair of good-quality slacks that feel comfortable and make you look thin. Now think about the three other pairs of slacks you never wear because they wrinkle too much, make you look fat, and don't go with any jackets you have. Where *is* that Goodwill clothing donation bag?

If we're honest, most of us are less than vigilant in following the one-to-three rule of acquisitions to donations. (We're working on that.) But to be fair, a lot of the clutter is stuff we didn't even ask for, like the constant stream of "junk" mail. How did those companies know where to find us? Who told them about our buying habits, our secret longing to have more hair on our head and less fat around our middle? Masters of persuasion, they seduce us with promises of a better life, more energy, heightened mental capacity, and millions of dollars in unearned income. They are slick, convincing, and relentless. Besides, we have to go through all the mail just in case there's a bill, a check, or something from ASCD in there somewhere. By the time we figure out who is selling our mailing address to whom, it's too late. We sign up for one credit card, and 20 other companies make us offers. We subscribe to one magazine, and a dozen others rush to inform us that we need theirs as well. And pity the person who ever buys one item of clothing, one piece of software, or one bottle of vitamins through the mail: these companies make more money selling our names and addresses than they do on the products we purchase!

In order to put a stop to junk mail, you have to take a proactive approach. When you sign up for a new credit card or magazine subscription or purchase anything through the mail, be emphatic about the fact that you do not want your name or contact information loaned, sold, or shared in any way, within their company or with any third party. If you purchase something from a mail-order catalog, the only way to stop future mailings is to call the customer service department and explicitly request to be removed from the mailing list. You can use the time you spend on hold to go through the rest of your junk mail; use a speakerphone if you have one, as it will save stress on your neck and shoulders. If the company has your phone number, fax, or e-mail, remember to ask them to expunge those as well.

If all else fails, sell your house and move. Fourth-class mail is not forwarded by the post office. (Lou has moved every 2 years for most of his life; Lynell has been at the same home for the past 27 years. Enough said.)

Organizing Your Stuff

We recommend assigning items you've already accumulated and decided you must keep to one of three types of spaces: display, convenient storage, and long-term storage.

Display Spaces

As our Feng Shui advisor pointed out, display spaces catch the eye when you walk into a room: the counter or bench under the bay window, the dresser top, the kitchen or dining room table, the table in the entry hall, the bathroom counter. These should be 90 percent clear, with 10 percent of the space devoted to items that are beautiful, whimsical, inspirational, memorable, and meaningful to you and the people who share your space. Choose flowers, photos, statues, candles, stuffed animals, decorative boxes, carvings, and other items that add color and warmth and make you smile when you see them. Do they give you energy rather than draining you when you look at them? Do they speak to you of love or hope? Do they encourage you? Then they belong on display.

Some display spaces, such as countertops and tabletops, can serve as convenient workspaces for quick sorting and processing tasks, such as folding clothes, collating papers, and eating meals. The key is to use these spaces only for tasks or projects you can complete fairly quickly; in a display space, today's unfinished project becomes tomorrow's nagging clutter. Before reading on, try answering the questions in Figure 4.2.

Convenient Storage Spaces

These include the top drawers in a desk or base cabinet, the waist-high drawer in a file cabinet, and the two feet in the center of the closet

4.2 Pause and Apply

Think about the potential display spaces—the prime real estate—in your classroom. What catches your eye (and the eyes of your students) upon entering the room? Do the colors and the items say, "Welcome! In this place, you are loved. You are capable and full of promise"? Or are there piles of "stuff" that overwhelm you and make you and your students feel like you could never get through it all no matter how hard you tried? Is it obvious what is important—what is treasured—in your classroom? Are the items on display relevant to your current projects and curriculum focus? Does every item contribute to a nurturing learning environment?

nearest the door. As the Realtors say, three things determine the value of a property: location, location, location. These convenient storage spaces are extremely valuable because of their prime location. They are the ideal places for items you use frequently but that would look like clutter if left on the tops of counters and tables. At home, these items would include toiletries, kitchen gadgets, clothing, and mail; at school, think supplies, memos, gradebooks, and student assignments. But what if these spaces are already full? All too often, when this happens, they "force" the most frequently used items back out onto the display spaces where they look like—you guessed it—clutter. The exercise in Figure 4.3 will help you to assess your use of convenient storage space.

Long-Term Storage Spaces

You saved money buying a dozen reams of paper, but do you need all twelve reams on the counter? Of course not; what you don't use goes into long-term storage. It is important, however, to go through your long-term storage areas on a regular basis. This serves a triple purpose: to make room for more relevant items, to help reinforce what's important to you as you decide what to keep and what to recycle, and to remind you to think

4.3 Pause and Apply

Take a moment to identify the convenient storage locations in your home, office, or classroom.

Inventory what is in those locations now. Are these things you use on a daily basis?

If not, where else could you put them? (Trash bin? Goodwill bag? Another storage location?)

Can you create a space for daily-use items that would be convenient to access in that location? Can you make room for five items you had been leaving on the counter or top of the desk or table? Do you feel like you just lost five pounds? (Yes, clutter weighs us down, at least on an emotional level.)

twice about storing anything in the first place. As Lynell's father often says, "Rather than collecting, filing, storing, and *then* tossing, it would be easier just to toss the stuff to start with." If that's out of the question for you, take a moment to consider the suggestions in Figure 4.4.

4.4 Pause and Apply

Make a list of the 10 things you consider the most important in your personal or professional life. If you are so inclined, type the list on your computer or print it out nicely, give it a title and frame it. As you sort through the clutter in your home or workplace, refer to the framed list as you decide what to keep or discard. Remember, it takes energy to keep things. Get rid of the things that are no longer relevant to make room for those things that are.

Remember, it's not about getting rid of everything; it's about getting rid of all those things that are not relevant to our sense of purpose in life. Clutter nags, and nagging causes stress. To relieve clutter stress, guard against influx and make sure your spaces are used appropriately to make your surroundings more uplifting and your work more efficient. Most importantly, make sure the items you choose to display reflect your sense of purpose and speak to you and those around you of love, encouragement, and hope. Stress cannot survive under those conditions.

5

The Busyness of Life

"I wouldn't be so stressed if I didn't have so much to do!"

How often have you heard those words? How often was it *you* saying them? As Henry David Thoreau once said, "It isn't enough to be busy. Ants are busy." The critical question is, "What are we busy about?" In his book *The Power of Purpose: Creating Meaning in Your Life and Work*, Richard J. Leider points out that in our society, "Busyness is a way of gaining approval for our self-worth. . . . But it is a nervous way of living because we continuously seek approval from outside ourselves. . . . We need to discover what part of busyness is just cultural consensus (i.e., norms we accept) and what part is an expression of our real purpose."[1]

How did we arrive at this point where we spend most of our waking hours at the office or on the road? We have a friend whose 9-year-old disguised himself as "Daddy" for Halloween. The costume? Laptop computer, cell phone, briefcase, and a garment bag! If your children, students, colleagues, or employees were to dress up as *you*, what would they be wearing? How would they accessorize the outfit? Is that how you would like to be seen?

Start with Dessert

Lynell's Uncle Chet always eats his dessert before the main course—just in case he runs out of room. While he may not have his nutritional priorities right, he provides a wonderful illustration of the old saying, "first things first."

In his workshops, Richard Bolles asks participants to make a list of what they would do if they just found out they had only two weeks to live. Others have suggested that we live life as though it were the day before leaving on vacation. While both of these approaches have merit, they emphasize getting things in order for someone else to take over when we're gone—whether temporarily or permanently. It's not that we have anything against delegation, but just for fun, imagine the flipside: what if you just got *back* from vacation only to find that you had another 100 years to live? Imagine! No hurry sickness or time pressure, but a sense of opportunity to embark on a powerfully effectual life.

You might decide to take the "gallon-jar approach" illustrated in *First Things First*, by Stephen Covey and Roger and Rebecca Merrill:

> I attended a seminar once where the instructor was lecturing on time. At one point, he said, "Okay, it's time for a quiz." He reached under the table and pulled out a wide-mouth gallon jar. He set it on the table next to a platter with some fist-sized rocks on it. "How many of these rocks do you think we can get in the jar?" he asked.
>
> After we made our guess, he said, "Okay. Let's find out." He set one rock in the jar . . . then another . . . then another. I don't remember how many he got in, but he got the jar full. Then he asked, "Is that jar full?"
>
> Everybody looked at the rocks and said, "Yes."
>
> Then he said, "Ahhh." He reached under the table and pulled out a bucket of gravel. Then he dumped some gravel in and shook the jar and the gravel went in all the little spaces left by the big rocks. Then he grinned and said once more, "Is the jar full?"
>
> By this time we were on to him. "Probably not," we said.
>
> "Good!" he replied. And he reached under the table and brought out a bucket of sand. He started dumping the sand in and it went in all the little spaces left by the rocks and the gravel. Once more he looked at us and said, "Is the jar full?"
>
> "No!" we all roared.
>
> He said, "Good!" and he grabbed a pitcher of water and began to pour it in. He got something like a quart of water in that jar. Then he said, "Well, what's the point?"
>
> Somebody said, "Well, there are gaps, and if you really work at it, you can always fit more into your life."
>
> "No," he said, "that's not the point. The point is this: if you hadn't put these big rocks in first, would you ever have gotten any of them in?"[2]

What are the "big rocks" in your life? Your family? Your loved ones? Your dreams? Time for yourself? Remember to put those in your jar first—not out of fear of running out of time or space, but from a clear sense of purpose and mission in your life.

The Business of Education

Administrators

We would propose that one of the "big rocks" for school administrators is supporting staff with professional development. If we are truly in the business of education, we need to offer growth opportunities to our staff as well as our students.

Compare the approaches of the following two assistant superintendents. The *first* looked for new projects and programs that might appeal to the directors, coordinators, and supervisors who reported to her. She would call these individuals into her office to discuss the opportunity, and if they loved the idea, she would help them find the training necessary for the job. She joked that sometimes she trained people so well they could leave for better jobs, but she was willing to take that risk. The *other* assistant superintendent would take a stack of papers and a wad of Post-it notes into his office and shut the door. A hush would fall over the department—employees knew the drill. An hour later, he would emerge and instruct his secretary to distribute the stack of papers, each bearing a Post-it with an employee's name on it. If you didn't like your assignment, you could look for another job—he was willing to take *that* risk.

Lynell recently had the privilege of meeting with the superintendent of the Peninsula School District in Gig Harbor, Washington. Jim Coolican recounted how important he believed it was to invest in his teachers. When he heard about a master's degree in instructional technology that could be earned onsite throughout his district, he presented the idea to his staff. The response? A standing ovation. Teachers currently in the program are thrilled to be able to earn a master's degree without having to drive across the Narrows Bridge with its omnipresent traffic jams. Another benefit of the program is that it requires teams of colleagues to work together on projects. The mutual support and friendships that evolve out of this work have helped lower the stress that frequently comes with the introduction of new technologies. For Jim's teachers, the program has been a godsend and a good incentive to stay with the district.

Another big issue for school administrators has been information management. A study of principals and superintendents by the opinion-research group Public Agenda paints a picture of school leaders who want to improve their schools but feel that the emphasis placed on bureaucracy and paperwork keeps them from focusing on student learning. Eighty-eight percent of the superintendents and 83 percent of the principals in the study thought there were too many mandates and too few funds to carry them out. Fifty-four percent of superintendents and 48 percent of principals said they had to work around the system to get things done; only a third of superintendents and 30 percent of principals said that the system helped them advance their goals. According to 81 percent of the superintendents and 47 percent of the principals, concern over bureaucracy and the politics of their jobs has led colleagues to leave the profession.[3]

A similar study by the National Association of Secondary School Principals, released in November 2001, found that high school principals felt they had too little time and too much paperwork to do. Seventy percent of the respondents said that lack of time was the biggest hurdle in their work, while 69 percent mentioned too much paperwork.[4]

In order to survive information overload, more and more site- and district-level administrators are turning to technology to automate time-consuming processes. The most successful approaches to managing information start by building a systemic hierarchy of informational priorities. (Please contact the authors for more information about this type of approach.)

Teachers

In talking to teachers (and working as teachers ourselves), we have identified the following top three complaints about the profession:

1. **Wildly diverse ability and experience levels among students in the same class.** So you're teaching 4th grade this year? Out of 24 students, you might have three who read at a 9th grade level or above, seven who can almost read at grade level, 10 who read at a 2nd grade level, and four who speak no English or cannot read at all. You'll have to tutor some of the kids before school, some during recess, more during lunch, and others after school. You'll send extra work home for the parents to do with the kids at night, and you'll try to get volunteers to come in for more individualized reading practice when you do breakout groups in the afternoon. You'll have 5th graders come in for cross-age tutoring as often as their teacher allows. Are you *sure* today isn't Friday?

2. **Impossibly long workdays, yet not enough time to prepare for lessons, correct papers, etc.** You want to create a compelling multimedia presentation to introduce a unit on Seminole Indians. You promised your family you'd go to the beach with them on Sunday afternoon. But by the time you finish putting the lesson together, not only have you missed church but you also had to skip the beach. And you never did get to that dirty laundry that appears to be reproducing in the bedroom closets.

   Maybe we should just skip the Seminoles this year? How many content standards are we meeting with this lesson anyway? Even Robert Marzano, a leader in the standards movement, admits: "To cover all the content in the standards identified thus far, you would have to change schooling from K–12 to K–22."[5]
3. **Overwhelming pressures of standardized testing and other external accountability measures.** With all you want to teach the kids, how can you rationalize spending so much time preparing them to take a state-mandated test? How can this possibly help the kids who don't even speak English? Do you think our Thornburg Center associate Gary Stager might have a point with his "Pencils Down" movement? Really, what could the state, the testing companies, and the manufacturers of No. 2 pencils do if we all just refused to administer the tests? We are not talking revolution, insolence, or insubordination; we are simply declaring our right to ask one simple question: "Why?"

   Of course, most educational mandates and policies are designed with good intentions. Problems arise when politicians and bureaucrats start to prescribe ways to carry out those intentions. When we focus on "how" and lose sight of "why," education changes from a way of *empowering* teachers and students to a system of *enforcing* mandates and policies. Always remember to ask yourself: why am I doing this? Why am I asking my students to do this? Once the purpose is clear, the procedures (and the resources to carry out those procedures) will fall into place.

   Doubtful? Here are a couple of real-life examples from Lynell's experience as a French teacher at Stanford University:

Correcting papers. I assumed that Stanford students would turn in fastidiously perfect work. That did happen, on occasion. But for the most part, the French homework came in looking as though puppies had used it for teething. With 24 students' papers to correct, I was up until 2:00 a.m. every morning, using up red pen after red pen writing corrections on every page. I began to think of myself as a dedicated teacher on the fast track to martyr status. Eighty hours a week? Of course. That's what dedicated teachers have to spend to do a good job. Or is it?

Let's not admit how long it took for me to figure this one out. Let's just say that one night, I started to wonder why *I* was writing out the correct responses on grammar exercises 24 times when it was the *students* who needed the practice. I decided then and there to correct the first 10 mistakes on each paper and then draw a line across the page. Students who wanted their papers corrected to the end would have to be more careful and not "waste" their allotted errors on careless mistakes. From then on, as if by magic, no student ever made more than 10 mistakes per assignment!

What about written compositions? Some, if not most, of my students were incredibly creative, even with a limited French vocabulary. Instead of just correcting their work and returning the papers, it occurred to me, why not use their compositions as a way of reinforcing vocabulary and grammar in a context that was much more entertaining and relevant than the examples in the textbook? One student had written a particularly delightful story, and I decided to project it for the whole class to see the next day. The student, obviously quite proud to have been chosen, could not resist coming up after class to complain. In the best French he could muster, he announced with a big grin that his lawyer would be calling. His point was well taken. After that, students were warned that—with their permission—their papers might be shared.

Creating and administering tests. Stanford required student grades to be based largely on midterms and final exams. The good news is that they did not yet require standardized testing, so I still had the option of using tests as positive learning experiences. I thought it might be interesting to have the students create the exams themselves. Why not invite them to say what *they* thought was important in the course and to design test questions accordingly?

I divided the class into four groups. Each group had to write an exam and make six copies of it for another group of students to take. Each student got two grades: one for writing and one for taking a test. Everyone did extremely well on both counts. For once they hadn't crammed; instead, they'd thoughtfully reviewed the course material, focusing on what they thought was most important to learn and retain from the class.

The problem with most formal assessments is that they take all the joy out of a good test. Kids *love* tests that are designed to show their mastery. They even have a word for such tests: they call them "games."

Empowering teaching assistants. Who ever came up with the insane paradigm of one (relatively) old teacher working while 20–30 (relatively) young students watch? If anything, shouldn't it be the other way around? But wait, we can flip that classroom upside down. Ah, that's better: now the teacher who gets paid to come to class has a free, dedicated "staff" of 20–30 young people who, by law, must show up for "work."

The teacher, gifted with insight, intuition, and the big-picture view of what needs to be learned in the class, must search for strengths, passions, and potential. The fun begins as she uncovers talent in the most unlikely places: students with unexcused absences, discipline problems, limited English, poor academic records, or aggressive or withdrawn behavior patterns. She empowers these students by asking them to help others.

In technology-enriched classrooms, teachers can adopt the model of our friend Steve Dworetzky, from Martin Luther King Middle School in Los Angeles. Steve calls it "Ask Three Before Me." He makes a list of all the technical skills needed in the class and invites three or four volunteers to learn each of the skills—operating the scanner, resizing images in Photoshop, creating PowerPoint slideshows, and so on. When students are working on projects, they are allowed to ask Steve a question only if they have the names of three student experts they've already interrogated. Steve claims this frees him up to attend conferences without the students even noticing that he's gone!

Students

The further most people distance themselves from age 4 (when children ask "Why?" a hundred times a day), the more they fall into the mindless rut of day-to-day activities and the more they see each activity as an end in itself rather than as a means to a greater end. Albert Einstein explained that he was able to discover the theory of relativity only because he continued to ask questions, like a child. When we, as parents or teachers, start to lose patience with a seemingly endless stream of questions, we should keep in mind that it is within our power to encourage or discourage potential Einsteins.

When students ask, "Why do we have to learn this?" they are sending us two extremely important messages: that *they care about context*, and that *we haven't established the context in a way that makes sense to them*. (Another way of expressing this would be to ask, "How relevant is this material to the students' lives, interests, goals, and experience?")

Some of the more entertaining illustrations of the importance of context were Johnny Carson's "Carnac the Magnificent" skits on the "Tonight Show." Johnny's sidekick, Ed McMahon, would read an answer, to which Johnny would "divine" the question. Here's a classic example:

> Ed: "Siss, boom, baa."
> Johnny: "What's the sound made by an exploding sheep?"

What role does context play in helping students learn and recall information? Remember the spelling lists kids took home in elementary school? There were 25 new words every week. Why those words and not others? Instead of the daunting task of *25,000 different words* to learn, why not focus on *100 spelling patterns*? Why not start with children's songs and show how words that rhyme often have similar spelling?

We all learn by connecting new information to ideas, facts, and feelings that are already stored in our brains. Students need to know how questions and answers fit together; otherwise, the curriculum becomes decontextualized, meaningless busywork. Random lists of spelling words, pages of math drill and practice, and mere collections of historical dates and figures are all examples of decontextualized curriculum. Both teaching and learning become rote, mechanical, and lifeless under these conditions.

From Busyness to Business

Administrators, teachers, and students can all get buried in the busyness of education. But as we go through our school days from task to task, from obligation to obligation, let's remember to pause and ask ourselves, "Why am I doing this?" If there is no good answer, let's take a bold new approach. Let's just scratch it off our to-do list *without doing it*. We are much too busy with the real business of education to waste our time on such busyness.

6

Affording the Possibilities

When was the last time you heard an educator say, "No, really, I couldn't take another dollar"? Ask Dennis Bruno, superintendent of the Glendale School District in Flinton, Pennsylvania, about attitude and money.

"I knew we needed money, so I just wrote grant proposals and asked for it," he says. "I often got more than I asked for. Solving the stress of money problems is more about attitude than actual dollars. The first 2 grants were hard; the next 13 were easy."

What we appreciate about this attitude is that it doesn't consider the cost of doing what needs to be done for kids; it considers the cost of *not* doing it!

So How Can I Afford It?

In his bestseller *Rich Dad, Poor Dad*, Robert Kiyosaki tells how he grew up in Hawaii with two "fathers": his own dad, a well-educated but relatively poor college professor, and his best friend's dad, a wealthy businessman. Kiyosaki writes:

> Rich dad forbade the words "I can't afford it." (In my real home, that's all I heard.) Instead, he required his children to say, "How can I afford it?" His reasoning, the words "I can't afford it" shut down our brain. It didn't have to think anymore. "How can I afford it?" opened up the brain, forcing it to think and search for answers . . . [bringing up] possibilities, excitement, and dreams.[1]

Poor teachers, schools, and districts say things like, "Everything is just too expensive. It's so stressful to work without the tools we need for the job. How can they expect us to?" Creative educators, on the other hand, love to play with the possibilities: "How can we make this happen for our kids?"

Shopping for Bargains

When it comes to economizing, educators are hard to beat: we can squeeze 10 cents from a nickel, art lessons out of used egg cartons, and math drills from discarded Popsicle sticks. (See Figure 6.1 for other ways to save money in schools.) But sometimes we are so focused on saving money that we buy things just because they are "such a good deal." The ultimate cost of jumping on such bargains is that we're stuck with resources that are inadequate for the needs they were purchased to meet. We end up spending much more to fix that shortfall later than it would have cost to buy the right products and services in the first place.

6.1 Pause and Apply

Do you belong to an organization that is already purchasing equipment at special discount pricing? (Universities often negotiate special pricing on laptops, for example.)

What other groups, associations, or institutions do you belong to that could purchase in volume? How do you think that volume would impact the price per unit? Could you be instrumental in launching such a purchase agreement?

Shopping can be deceiving. It masquerades as harmless fun, or even a productive way to spend a couple of hours. But spending money we don't have on things we don't need to store in cupboards that are already full is more than a harmless habit—it is an insidious stressor. Lynell used to laugh when her husband would throw the credit card bills on the floor in mock protest and exclaim, "The *nerve* of those people!" When she would ask, "But didn't you *buy* all that stuff?" he had to reply, "Well, yeah. But I could probably take some of it back."

Does this sound like anyone you know? If you feel stressed out by a lack of time and money, think again about how you shop, either at home or at work. Are you proactive? Do you make lists? Do you buy things you *want* or things you *need*? There is a good reason that the best marketing executives make a lot of money. They possess an extremely lucrative skill: convincing us that we *need* what they entice us to *want*. Next time a vendor shows you a whiz-bang new product or you see something tempting in a catalog, evaluate it not on the *features*—"it slices, it dices, it dances, it sings"—but on the *benefits* it offers your students. If you think of features as *wants* and benefits as *needs*, what you really need to purchase becomes much clearer. Try the example in Figure 6.2 to see how *you* define wants and needs in your life.

6.2 Pause and Apply

Take a look in your closet at school. What have you purchased on impulse solely because you were tempted by the bargain price? Did it turn out to be a good investment? What items did you spec out ahead of time? ("How does this fit with my existing curriculum? How does it meet the needs of my struggling students? How does it complement and enhance the work of my advanced students who need a challenge?")

If you are applying for grants, ask for support for real *needs* (goods and services that you can show will clearly benefit students) and your appeal will be more compelling than if you simply put together a laundry list of *wants* ("99 computers with all the bells and whistles because, well, they're really cool!"). A young boy in India clearly understood this concept when he approached Lynell and asked if she was a teacher. When Lynell nodded, he stuck out his hand and smiled knowingly as he begged for money to buy "pens for school." Who could resist that kind of targeted appeal?

Show Me Your Checkbook

There is a saying: "Show me your checkbook, and I'll show you what you value in life." In career-planning or goal-setting workshops, we are often asked to speculate about what we'd do if we came into a great deal of money. Noted career and life counselor Nella Barkley and her colleagues at Crystal-Barkley Corporation have clients work through three exercises:

1. Imagine that a distant relative leaves you a fortune of at least $10 million. According to the will, you can spend the money only on yourself. Write down *in 10 minutes or less* how you would spend it.
2. The executor then says you have another $10 million to give to organizations or individuals. You have *10 minutes* to list recipients.
3. Now you're going to receive another $10 million, giving you total economic freedom. How would you spend a week? Take no more than *20 minutes* to write down exactly where and how you would spend the week. Then answer the same for a year.

The exact dollar amount is not the issue. *The critical factor in this exercise is the time allotted to make your spending choices*. It must be quick. (See Figure 6.3 for another budgeting exercise.)

6.3 Pause and Apply

Create two presentations using selected "real numbers" from the budget of a project you have worked on: one showing how well you have used the money, and another showing how the money was insufficient to meet your needs.

When you don't have time for calculators and spreadsheets, you will come up with your gut-level "intuitive" responses, explains Nella.[2] We tend to be at our most creative when we are in this mode. Besides, for most people, living life like a calculator is not only devoid of joy but also very stressful. There's always the fear of running short or making a mistake: we think of Lynell's father, who does the math in his head to check and make sure he hit the right keys on the calculator, or Lou, who jokes that he needs a travel visa to visit the "left" side of his brain (and it isn't always granted).

Both Sides Now

Today the model of left- and right-hemispheric specializations of the brain is scientifically recognized as too limited. Still, it remains very useful metaphorically to refer to the left side of the brain as that part of us that is concerned with self-preservation, crunches numbers, and warns us when it thinks resources become scarce. It fills us with fear and anxiety to make sure we don't do anything "crazy," and it loves to think it's in control because it's "dealing with the real numbers." The right side of the brain can quickly dispel this illusion with the simple exercise in Figure 6.4.

6.4 Pause and Apply

For a week—or even just a day—write down the whole sentence every time you catch yourself using the phrase: "I need. . . ." Go back and evaluate honestly how many times you actually meant "I want. . . ." Try this exercise with students at school (or teenagers at home) to reveal how much we are all influenced by advertising and addicted to shopping.

The same numbers can tell a very different story, depending on the intention of the storyteller. Consequently, the metaphoric left side of your brain is not the most accurate tool to measure your personal or professional well-being.

The creative side of our thinking needs no calculator because it deals in the nonnumeric currency of images, hopes, and dreams. It's the home of our truest self, the one that assures us that if we follow our passion, the resources will inevitably follow. Stress, fear, anxiety, disappointment, and despair cannot live in this positive atmosphere. The linear modality of the left side can do nothing but call this side names—"pie-in-the-sky," "unrealistic," "risky"—because it cannot comprehend it. Trying to measure a nonlinear world with a linear mind is like trying to measure the distance between stars by holding a ruler to the sky; the task is beyond its reach.

Our creative side refuses to do anything that isn't fun. Here lives the teacher who agrees to administer the standardized tests in her classroom but insists that the No. 2 pencils be replaced by crayons. Here thrives the administrator who responds to the state's latest unfunded mandates by saying:

> You'll be pleased to know that we are already doing many of the things you recommend. You are welcome to come and observe our work in action any time you feel the need to assess it. By the way, we have time *either* to fill out all the forms you so graciously sent *or* to teach the children. Please let us know if you disagree with our choice.

There is no end to the number of well-meaning friends, job exigencies, and day-to-day tasks and events that will draw us to the seemingly safer left side of the brain. (Realistically, that is where we need to be to balance our checkbooks.) But remember that the flights of fancy, flashes of genius, and real breakthroughs in our lives come when we escape the constraints and enjoy the freedom of our most creative selves.

Blame or Bliss

We can choose to live what Henry David Thoreau described as "lives of quiet desperation." We can blame the district office, the state, the federal government, the parents, society, the boss, our colleagues, the weather—you name it. We can expend all our energy scrambling for resources, being stressed out, and fighting back against systems that relatively unenlightened people are trying to enforce. *Or* we can live the abundant life: we can use the resources we do have more creatively and keep our focus on the highest purpose, the Big Picture, that gives meaning to our daily lives.

Money, like time, is relative. Putting together a budget when you are convinced you don't have enough money is a surefire recipe for stress, while putting together a budget for a noble mission you are committed to achieving is bound to result in success.

7

The People Principle

We've all heard the story of the principal showing off his new computer lab when the visitor asks, "But where are the students?" and the principal replies, "We found it easier to manage the lab without them."

If we tallied up the average day's challenges and irritations, *people* would usually outnumber *things*. Think about it. First there are the mildly annoying behaviors of casual friends, family, and colleagues:

- The teacher next door who complains about financial burdens: "What a pain to have all three of my kids at Harvard, even though they are all on full scholarships!"
- The cousin who criticizes her insensitive husband for sending only two dozen roses on their 30th anniversary: "You'd think the cheapskate could come up with a dozen per decade!"
- The friend who whines about her chores: "You wouldn't *believe* the amount of laundry I had to do after our two-week vacation to that luxury resort in Hawaii!"

Then there are the people we live or work with on a regular basis whose behavior seriously challenges our patience. On the worst of days, they remind us of the 1944 existentialist play *Huis Clos (No Exit)*, by French author Jean-Paul Sartre. The play describes three characters—a man (Garcin) and two women—who find themselves locked for all eternity in hell, which in their case is a living room. The most famous utterance in the play occurs when Garcin proclaims, "*L'enfer, c'est les autres*" (Hell is other people).[1]

If you were to choose a setting for a play about workplace "hell," what would it be? A boardroom? A staff room? A classroom? If there were only three characters in the play (and you were one of them), who would the other two characters be?

The next time you have the opportunity, try extending these hypothetical questions into a group activity. Divide participants into groups of three to six, and assign each group the task of writing a short skit called "The Staff Meeting." (Determine the number of lines of dialogue according to the amount of time you have to spend on the activity.) Suggest that the characters may or may not represent attendees at their last staff meeting but that they must represent the kind of people who could or would make those meetings a type of "hell." As the groups perform, notice any personality types that come up in more than one skit.

Now what if you wrote a play with *students* as the characters? As you know, most public schools don't get to choose which students to admit. In Tacoma, Washington, where Lynell grew up, there are neighborhoods whose gated mansions have mountain views and their own private lakes; there are other neighborhoods whose run-down shacks tumble onto streets where drive-by shootings are all too common.

Edison Elementary School stands out as a bright light in one of those latter neighborhoods. As the mission statement promises its students, "Edison is a friendly place where I can be safe, where I can learn many things, where I am respected, and where I can grow." The principal of the school, Ethel Wellington-Trawick, is there because she loves children, but every day presents its challenges. The children come to school with so much anger that fights break out with minimal provocation. Ethel was spending so much time settling disputes that she eventually developed a system to deal with them. All parties involved in a dispute come into her office, sit at a round table, and fill out a form to tell their side of the story. An example can be seen in Figure 7.1. Elisha and Jason were 4th graders in Miss Cuff's class. After reviewing each of their perspectives, Ethel held an arbitration session and made sure all three parties agreed on the proposed "Ending to the Story." (The poor spelling on the form tells a story of its own, of course.)

7.1 "My Side of the Story"

My Name: Elisha Date: 10/27/97

Teacher: Miss Cuff

Jasin was cuseing at me. Jasin nes ta lev me a lon and I will lev Hem a lon. I not men to Bet you. Jasin and you or lieing.

(Translation: "Jason was cussing at me. Jason needs to leave me alone, and I will leave him alone. I did not mean to beat you. Jason and you are lying.")

A Wounded People

While teaching English as a second language, Lynell had the privilege of working with hundreds of students who came to the United States from war-torn countries. In a 1998 conference presentation, she encouraged educators to offer such children the avenue of multimedia to share their feelings, which were often too painful for words. In the session, Lynell included original music and images reflecting her own recent loss of a loved one. When the presentation was over, dozens of people came to the stage with tears in their eyes to squeeze Lynell's hand, give a pat or a hug, and comment about loved ones *they* had lost. In the next day's mail, a beautiful letter arrived from a widowed professor who shared how she had raised five children alone after losing her husband. These are the people who smile and reply "fine" when asked the increasingly rhetorical question, "How are you doing?" In our society, it's okay to whine and moan about lack of time and money or about the irritating traits and behavior of colleagues, friends, and family, but it's not okay to expose wounds of any kind.

Susan Lark, one of the foremost authorities on preventive medicine, writes in her March 2002 *Lark Letter*: "Whether we lose a spouse, parent, child, or even a pet, grief takes its toll on our emotions and can negatively affect our health. This experience of loss is not limited to death. Many women suffer tremendous grief during divorce; or when their children leave for college, the armed forces, or work; and even when close family members or friends move far away from home."[2]

Lark goes on to say that grief frequently manifests itself in diseases such as cancer, pneumonia, and immune dysfunction. She reports that one study found the risk of death doubled for men and women in the seven to twelve months after the death of a spouse.[3]

What about the children? We can't stop thinking about the 2nd grader whose grandparents recently dropped him off at school saying, "Our son and the boy's mother are both in jail. We're moving to Florida. We just can't be bothered anymore."

How do children with these kinds of emotional wounds focus on learning? How can handing them a book they can't read possibly make it all better?

We can only imagine how terrifying it must be for young children who come into a U.S. school not speaking English. Even though they've never held a book or learned to read in their own language, they find themselves suddenly held to the same "standards" as children with thousands of hours of language experience who were already reading fluently above grade level on their first day of school.

Prescribed Treatment

Of course we want all children to learn to read and to acquire not only the basic skills but also a love of art and music and a healthy self-esteem that propels them into joyful, lifelong learning. But we should not turn that noble desire into an ignoble prescription.

George Reavis, assistant superintendent of the Cincinnati Public Schools from 1939 to 1948, wrote the following allegory, which he entitled "The Animal School":

> Once upon a time, the animals decided they must do something heroic to meet the problems of society, so they organized a school. They adopted an activity curriculum consisting of running, climbing, swimming, and flying. To make it easier to administer the curriculum, all the animals took all the subjects.

> The duck was excellent in swimming. In fact, he was better than his instructor. But he made only passing grades in flying and was very poor in running. Since he was slow in running, he had to stay after school as well as drop swimming in order to practice running. This was kept up until his webbed feet were badly worn and he was only average in swimming. But average was acceptable in school, so nobody worried about that except the duck.
>
> The rabbit started at the top of the class in running but had a nervous breakdown because of so much make-up work in swimming.
>
> The squirrel was excellent in climbing until he developed frustration in the flying class where his teacher made him start from the ground up instead of from the treetop down. He also developed a charley horse from overexertion and then got a C in climbing and a *D* in running.
>
> The eagle was a problem child and was disciplined severely. In the climbing class, he beat all the others to the top of the tree but insisted on using his own way to get there.[4]

Does this sound like a school you attended or perhaps a school where you taught? In Figure 7.2, which column best represents the system in which you are currently working? Which column creates more joy and less stress for both teachers and students?

7.2 Pause and Apply

Ask, "How smart are you?"	Ask, "How are you smart?"
Enforce conformity	Empower diversity
Judge/accuse	Counsel/encourage
Disparage	Edify
Tally mistakes	Learn from mistakes
Say "they"	Say "we"

One of the most accurate tests for teacher burnout is the "they/we" test. It is so simple that as yet, no educational testing company we know of has found a way to charge for it. Teachers just have to listen to the words they choose to share the day's experiences with family or friends. Compare the following statements:

1. "They couldn't concentrate this afternoon."
2. "We laughed until the tears started flowing!"
3. "They didn't want to learn anything I had to teach."
4. "We took turns adding words, humor, and twists to the story."
5. "They filled out today's worksheets while I corrected yesterday's."
6. "We all just gasped when we saw the first group's presentation!"

Do you see a pattern? Are "we" enjoying each other's company, or are "they" driving us crazy? It's really that simple. Words are powerful. Watch those pronouns!

By the way, the same "test" works for principals and teachers, superintendents and boards, schools and communities, and parents and children.

Two Graves and Some Prayer Beads

There's an old Chinese proverb that says, "If you're going to pursue revenge, you'd better dig two graves." Next time you catch yourself expressing resentment towards someone, dwell on that emotion just long enough to sense how it feels in your body. Check to see if your teeth and fists are clenched, your mouth and throat are dry, and your stomach is in a knot. "Okay," you might say. "But you don't know what that person did to me." Whatever it was (and we truly mean *anything*, from cutting you off in traffic to ending a relationship), if you are harboring resentment, you are compounding the injury by the harm you continue to inflict on your own body. If we each had an electromagnometer to measure the impact of resentment, if we could chart what it does to our body chemistry and to each of our cells, we would notice a red line marked "stress" and see that resentment is clearly over that line.

When you relinquish the desire for retribution, a huge burden will be lifted from your spirit. And besides, making humanity perfect is too big a job for humans. As Mahatma Gandhi pointed out, "If we practice an eye for an eye and a tooth for a tooth, soon the whole world will be blind and toothless." Consider also Max Lucado's observation: "Relationships don't thrive because the guilty are punished, but because the innocent are merciful."[5]

Do people like Lucado and Gandhi just decide one day that they are going to be forgiving, loving, and merciful to all people, even those who clearly don't deserve such generosity of spirit? Is it really as easy as fingering prayer beads and chanting affirmations? Can we just buy the beads and photocopy the affirmations? Would that suffice to change our own behaviors and outlook on life?

Think about it. How many mornings have you promised yourself that no matter what he or she does today, you are not going to let it upset you? How much willpower does it take to make that affirmation stick? (Tally your abandoned determinations, let alone your diet plans. Can you recall one New Year's resolution that lasted into February?)

Of Two Minds

In spite of all the self-help books we read and the motivational speeches we attend, the affirmations and meditations of our conscious, volitional minds only work about 20 percent of the time. Part of the problem is that the conscious mind is bound by time, with a short-term memory span of about 20 seconds. It also has limited processing power: the brain can handle only about 2,000 bits of information per second, which allows it to process one to three events simultaneously before it goes into a frenzy and yells "time out!" It lives mostly in the past ("should have"/"could have") and the future ("should"/"could").[6]

The subconscious mind, on the other hand, is in charge of all those bodily functions like digestion, breathing, and circulation that we usually take for granted. It can handle thousands of events simultaneously, process 4 billion bits of information per second, and transform challenging lessons into "no-brainer" abilities and understanding.[7] As psychotherapist Rob Williams jokes: "After what Freud said about the subconscious mind, most of us are reluctant to go there." Of course, Williams continues, "If we are going to effect any permanent change, that's where the trip will take us because that's where beliefs, habits, understanding, and values are stored."[8]

Yet sometimes it seems as though our subconscious mind has an unlisted number. Well, we've found it, and we'd like to give it to you. The easiest way to have a two-way conversation with your subconscious mind ɔ have words with it") is through a very simple tech- kinesiology, or muscle testing. Applied kinesiology is e strength of certain muscles to determine bodily responses to a wide range of questions. The process typically uses the deltoid muscle of the shoulder, with a tester pushing down on the arm of a subject who is asked to hold the arm rigid at shoulder level. Depending on what's being tested, the arm either stays strongly in place or drops in sudden weakness. The foremost pioneer of this process was George Goodheart, who explored the phenomenon extensively in the second half of the 20th century. He found that certain substances such as beneficial nutrients would cause muscle response to remain strong, while others, such as toxins, would immediately cause the muscle to weaken.

John Diamond published his landmark book on the topic, *Your Body Doesn't Lie: Unlock the Power of Your Natural Energy!*, in 1994.[9] Diamond shared extensive and highly replicable research that showed the remarkable efficacy of applied kinesiology in determining body responses not just to substances but also to emotional and intellectual stimuli. For example, he tested subjects' muscle strength in responding to statements such as "I love you" and "I hate you." With the former statement, the muscle remained strong; with the latter, it went weak.

Today there are numerous specialized applications of muscle testing. Educational kinesiology, for example, is probably best known in the work of BrainGym, which uses muscle testing to help prepare the mind and emotions for optimal performance. (Rob Williams's work in psychological kinesiology evolved from educational kinesiology.)

This is not metaphysical speculation. Today, applied kinesiology is a well-established practice used primarily by health care professionals. In its most daring uses, it is applied with some astonishing results to psychological processes and even to the study of human consciousness itself.

In his video with Bruce Lipton called *The Biology of Perception/The Psychology of Change*,[10] Rob Williams tells of a woman who came to one of his workshops after 15 years of conventional psychotherapy. She assured him that she had completely worked through the issues she had due to an abusive mother. When he muscle tested her about her mother, her arm dropped like a wet noodle. Whoops. You can't pull the wool over the eyes of your subconscious. It knows what you are feeling, intimately, in every fiber of your being. To use a computer analogy, negative emotions are like nasty viruses corrupting our memories, hacking into our operating systems.

Right Relationships

So how do we heal relationships? Author/therapist Karol Truman suggests starting with 490 forgivenesses. (She does the math from the biblical passage Matthew 18:22, where Jesus tells Peter to forgive an offender 7 × 70 times.) Truman proposes that we take a big notepad and a pen or pencil, sit down, and write out the following:

> I, [your name], forgive [his/her name] for [the offense in question] and release [him/her] to [his/her] highest good.

She counsels that for best results, we continue this process until 490 forgivenesses are issued. There might be one particularly painful incident, person, or feeling that will need to be written out 2, 10, or even 60 times until the negative energy dissipates. Once it does, you can move on to another incident. Truman recommends starting with our parents—who, however unintentionally, are often the biggest offenders—and then moving on to other emotionally "charged" people and events in our lives. Every forgiveness lifts the vibrational frequency in every one of the trillions of cells in our bodies.[11] The subconscious "knows" when those energy shifts occur, and we can ask it to check for us (did I *really* forgive him?) using applied kinesiology. As the title of Truman's earlier book indicates, *Feelings Buried Alive Never Die*.

Loves Me, Loves Me Not

Remember the little game we played as children where we took a flower and pulled off the petals one by one, saying, "Loves me, loves me not"? All the while, we were hoping that when the last petal came off, it would be "Loves me." Actually, we might do better to ask the flower if it loves itself. According to pretty much every insightful philosopher, theologian, and therapist who has ever walked the earth, you can't love anyone else unless you love yourself first. Maya Angelou quotes the African proverb, "Be careful when a naked person offers you a shirt."[12]

When we want to make a change in our life, that change must be accomplished from the inside out. By internalizing this principle, Truman writes, "We can create a shift of major proportions, both in our feeling nature and in the way we view and approach life. This consciousness shift can bring about an effortless surrender of judging and blaming others for conditions in which we find ourselves. Because *they* (whoever we have been blaming) did not *create* our challenges, *they* cannot *fix* them."[13]

The Victim Mentality

As long as we see ourselves as *victims* (stressed out, hopeless, helpless, and powerless), we will continue to surround ourselves with victimizers. It's common knowledge that women who were abused by their fathers tend to marry abusive men. Logically, one would think they would "know better" and only consider a kind and gentle mate. But there is a different kind of "logic" operating here, one that says, "Clearly I *am* a victim, so I should be treated like one."

When we operate with a victim mentality at the subconscious level, we invite other people and forces to control our lives; we attract people and situations that make our lives difficult. So what do we do to let go of a victim mentality? At the heart of this pattern is *uncontrolled reaction*. Being a victim of circumstances means being only reactive, responding to stimuli as a force of habit: "This happened, there's nothing I can do about it, that's life." Reactive thought sees no way to control situations; it can only respond, most commonly with angry resignation that fosters resentment, which in turn sustains the sense of helplessness. We leave victimhood with a perceptual shift, from seeing circumstances as limiting or controlling factors to understanding that we have far more power than we realized. That power begins with seeing that we have the ability to control our reactions. Once we begin to proactively choose our responses to situations, we quickly come to see that events have no power in and of themselves. They're not intrinsically good or bad; we place them in one of those categories by assigning them a reactive meaning. Exercising proactive control of our ability to reassign meaning to events leads us into enormous personal freedom. From there, we learn that we can choose the overall compass setting of our lives and always remain true to it. If the prow of our ship is tossed about by waves and we're knocked off course a bit here and there, we can always steer back to our true heading. We let go of cursing the waves for their personal attacks and reflections on our capabilities and innate human worth.

Roles People Play

As we started applying the principles in this book to our own lives in the course of our research, something delightful began to happen. One day last September, Lynell said to Lou, "It feels like we've been sprayed with jerk repellant. We just can't seem to meet anyone who isn't wonderful!"

You know the kind of people we mean:

- The neighbor who stores your off-season clothes in her guest room when you move to a place with smaller closets. (Thanks, Marian.)
- The girlfriends who arrive early for morning walks so that they can pull a few weeds in your front yard. (Thanks, Shan. Thanks, Nada.)
- The chiropractor who is so kind that your spine adjusts itself in anticipation of his healing touch. (Thanks, Dr. Rob.)

Sartre said *hell* is other people. Could the same be true of *heaven*? Imagine an environment where everyone was the kind of person you'd like to be with for all eternity—the Marians, the Shans and Nadas, with a Dr. Rob on every corner. Before reading any further, consider the exercise in Figure 7.3.

7.3 Pause and Apply

If you were to create a skit about a heaven with just you and two other people, what would those two other people be like? Make a list of their characteristics. (Remember, you'll be together for a long, long time, so avoid anything that would grate on your nerves!)

If you are a classroom teacher, consider asking your students to complete this exercise as well. It's a wonderful way for them to identify what they value!

Did you pattern your bunkmates after celebrities, such as Miss America, an Academy Award–winning actor, a Super Bowl champion, a Nobel Prize winner, or the world's richest man? Were there any unsung heroes on your list? Former teachers? Faithful friends? Did they have smiles on their faces and laughter and kindness in their hearts? Were they helpful and friendly and able to inspire you and make you feel good about yourself?

What characteristics of your hypothetical "heavenly" friends do *you* possess? If you exuded all those characteristics, could you create your own heaven on earth? If the latest biological theories are correct and we surround ourselves with people who conform to our view of reality, what kinds of friends and colleagues would you attract here and now?

We truly believe that the one sure-fire way to make other people better is to become better people *ourselves*. We are experiencing it in our own lives, and would love to see it happen in our schools. Imagine 20 applicants for every teaching and administrative job and perfect attendance by every child, just because everyone wants to be in that heavenly place called school! We don't mean a place where everyone is angelic and walks around sporting a halo. We are talking about saints "in training" who are still learning from their mistakes and who still exhibit enough human foibles to be called "characters." But they are all completely devoted and dedicated to offering themselves and each other unconditional love and encouragement, making sure that each and every person leaves school at the end of each day more energized and more hopeful than when they arrived.

8

Good Vibrations

Though the Beach Boys are best known as a surfer band, they were also pretty good biotherapists. We still feel those "Good Vibrations."

Unfortunately, however, we can also feel not-so-good vibrations. Whatever their nature, we constantly sense vibrations all around us. This is neither musical hype nor metaphysical mumbo jumbo; it's quite literally true, and is increasingly borne out by cutting-edge science. Why are these findings important? At worst, vibrations can dramatically alleviate stress; at best, they help prevent it altogether.

You might say that life is a "moving" experience: subatomic elements are constantly whizzing around at incomprehensible speeds and performing feats that defy logic as we once knew it. Quantum physics has had to rush new terms and concepts into play to describe events that refuse to accommodate themselves to standard Newtonian physics. In this chapter, we explore how some of these bold new scientific concepts play out in music, words, and even in the human heart.

The Sound of Music

Music is known to have properties that enhance learning and alter moods. The "mind-alert/body-relaxed" use of music, pioneered by Bulgarian psychiatrist Georgi Lozanov, uses rhythm to slow down bodily functions and high frequencies to charge the brain. Indeed, music has long been used by casual listeners and health-care professionals alike to calm nerves and experience the pleasure of sound. But just as there is the beauty of a favorite soft and gentle melody, there is also the screeching of fingernails on the blackboard. The fact is that sound can be either greatly empowering or highly toxic depending on how it's used. This is why we do workshops focused solely on what we call the purposeful use of music.

Psychoacoustics

French physician and psychologist Alfred Tomatis, called by some the "Einstein of the ear," was an early pioneer in the development of psychoacoustics—the study of the effects of sound on the central nervous system. Working through much of the latter half of the 20th century, Tomatis discovered that sound is actually a neurological nutrient that charges the neocortex of the brain.[1] We can, of course, survive without these sounds, but *with* them, our higher-order thinking skills become greatly enhanced; conversely, Tomatis discovered, other kinds of sounds can damage or discharge energy from the body.

What distinguishes healthful sounds from unhealthful ones? One of the most critical considerations is the rate or *frequency* at which the sound vibrates. Because sound is carried on waves, the vibration of sound is measured by determining the speed of one sound wave or cycle per second. This unit of measurement is known as a *hertz*. The musical note A, for example, vibrates at a frequency of 440 cycles per second, or 440 hertz. The normal range of hearing for humans is generally between 20 and 20,000 hertz, although some people can hear beyond that range, as can many animals, including dogs, dolphins, alligators, and elephants.

Everything physical—from people to the earth itself—has a frequency at which it most naturally vibrates. This is its *resonant frequency*. When we hear sounds that do not resonate with us, we get a vague sense of discomfort on one extreme to outright illness on the other. So what are the sounds that our brains thrive on? What exactly are those vibrations? According to the research of Tomatis, they include higher frequencies of sound: 80 percent of the neuroreceptors for sound respond only to frequencies above 3,000 hertz, and one-third of the charge that the ear supplies to the brain comes from these frequencies. Tomatis discovered that frequencies above 8,000 hertz provide enormous neurological benefit to the brain. To put this into some perspective, consider that typical human conversation ranges between 750 and 3,000 hertz.[2] Optimal frequencies for charging the neocortex, then, are well above what we hear in our usual working day.

Ranges of human hearing influence different areas of our lives. Low frequencies—between 125 and 750 hertz—greatly influence the vestibular system and, therefore, have the greatest impact on the body. Human languages usually operate at midrange frequencies—750 to 4,000 hertz—

although some use frequencies up to 12,000 hertz. Frequencies of 8,000 hertz and higher are the ones that best energize the nervous system.[3]

Unfortunately, we live in a world that is largely unaware of the power of sound. Have you heard cars rolling down the street with the bass turned up loud enough to stun small animals a hundred yards away? Our friend Joshua Leeds, one of the most knowledgeable and dynamic presenters we've encountered on the topic of psychoacoustics, calls such bass-heavy music "sonic Valium."[4] This is because extended exposure to loud bass sounds tends to discharge cerebral energy, thereby dulling the physical senses. "In areas like inner cities," Joshua recently told us, "kids want sound that will chill them out. Heavy bass does that." Joshua's concern for what he calls secondhand sound has led to the forefront of a new movement called "sonic activism."

"It really is time to deal with secondhand sound in much the same way that we've come to deal with secondhand smoke," Joshua told us. "I urge people to reclaim their sound space. People should determine for themselves what sounds are healthy and pleasing to them. There are just too many other people out there impacting my nervous system with sound. We live in a culture that's been filled with garbage noise, all kinds of unhealthy sound stimuli. Sound becomes empowering or not as we consciously use it or fail to. It's time for us to control how we take in sound as a nutrient."

When we consult with schools about their music use, one of the first things we do is to check music playback systems everywhere in the building. The bass is almost always far heavier than it should be. Keeping the bass in proper balance is critically important to prevent physical burnout, especially for teachers who have music playing most of the school day (and perhaps continue to listen to it on their own time). Likewise, it's important to keep the upper frequencies turned up as high as the playback system will allow while still keeping the music pleasant. Reaching this balance often requires outside ears, because most people's sense of sonic balance itself is out of optimal balance; few people realize how toxic their listening habits have become. (A number of psychoacousticians are available for consultation, though they can be hard to locate. Readers interested in contacting such a professional may contact the authors.)

Because we're both musicians as well as educational consultants, we're constantly asked by teachers, "What music should we play in the classroom?" This question is often posed with trepidation. Many educators fear a tense showdown with students (or even with each other) over issues of personal musical taste or cultural preference. We're always delighted to be able to completely defuse that concern. The answer gracefully skirts all such issues, because it has to do almost entirely with psychoacoustics.

Any music that provides optimal neurological nutrients is acceptable in the classroom. Ideally, that means music recorded, mixed, and mastered with a high percentage of high acoustic frequencies and played with the best frequency balance possible. Interestingly, music tends to self-organize by broad categories when considered from a psychoacoustics perspective; for example, classical music is generally more healthful sonically than are many forms of contemporary popular music.

Even governmental agencies have come to realize the significance of psychoacoustics and have used their properties to remarkable benefit. The city of Vallejo, California, attracted international attention in the winter of 2001 when it started playing certain kinds of music over speakers in high petty-crime districts. The crime rate in these areas plummeted dramatically—"some 25 to 40 percent at the bus transfer station," according to Mark Mazzaferro, public information officer for the city. "We saw similar programs used successfully in New York, Montreal, and Boston, so we decided to give it a try here. At the bus station, the only thing that changed was the music." The program cost all of about $200 per site. "We just went down to Target and bought a CD player, speakers, and CDs," Mazzaferro told us. "It was enough to do the job." People whose ears are psychoacoustically accustomed to particular musical properties have a very hard time tolerating sound that does not match those properties.

Listening habits can of course be changed, and there are numerous programs designed to do just that. Such programs can recondition the ears, first to discern the higher, healthier frequencies, and then to listen to them enjoyably. Some of these programs have demonstrated astonishing benefits for people suffering from a huge range of difficulties, from severe depression to autism. In our experience, the best of these is the Listening Program from Advanced Brain Technologies.[5]

The Sound of Words

When listening to music, exchanges between Lou and Lynell often go something like this:

Lynell: "Weren't those beautiful lyrics?"

Lou: "The song had *words*?"

Lou feels the power of songs primarily in the melody; Lynell sees the melody more as a vehicle to carry the words. When words create a vivid image or tell a compelling story, they can grip and even transport the listener. As an ESL teacher, Lynell used popular and classical music to create meaning and context for teaching real language to students. As we have learned from the research of Howard Gardner and authors like Thomas Armstrong, we can reach every learner when we offer instruction that draws upon multiple intelligences. When we present a slideshow with full-screen images plus a catchy melody and good lyrics, we are tapping the students' linguistic, musical, and visual intelligences at the same time—a sure-fire recipe for engaging the learner!

And just as Lynell and other educators have chosen particular songs for their rich vocabulary, they can also choose them for their emotional content, which can be carried by the words and melody. These selections change the atmosphere and the mood in the classroom almost instantaneously. For example, more and more teachers play classical or instrumental music before tests to calm their students' nerves. We recommend playing music when students enter the classroom to signal the transition between the energy levels of recess, lunch, or passing between classes and the more focused attention required in the classroom learning environment.

We also recommend explicit discussions with students about the power of music. We don't mean arguments over the merits of classical music versus rap, but rather talking about how advertisers and movie producers understand and use music as a communications tool. Students and teachers need to be able to make conscious choices about the music they listen to and understand the effect of those choices. In our workshops, we play a series of three instrumental clips and ask the audience to describe their feelings in response to each selection. The audience members consistently describe a transition from "energized" to "soothed," and from "soothed to "inspired," in a matter of less than three minutes.

In order to convey how lyrics can create instant "experiences," we have our workshop audiences do a little exercise using the titles of country-and-western songs. As Harlan Howard once put it, "Country music is three chords and the truth." Clearly, some of the most colorful expressions in the English language can be found in that unique musical genre, as is evident in Figure 8.1.

8.1 Pause and Apply

This makes a great group activity for adults as well as intermediate or high school students. Have each group of 3–6 participants choose any 12–15 of the song titles listed below. Their assignment is to use the words in those titles to create a story in letter, poem, or narrative style. They can use partial titles, and they can add up to 20 connector words. The final composition must be between 100 and 125 words. Each small group will have the opportunity to present its work to the large group.

Song Titles

- All My Exes Live in Texas
- Am I Double-Parked by the Curbstone of Your Heart?
- Billy Broke My Heart at Walgreens, and I Cried All the Way to Sears
- Bubba's Inconvenience Store
- Don't Believe My Heart Can Stand Another You
- Don't Strike a Match (to the Book of Love)
- Guess My Eyes Were Bigger Than My Heart
- Here's a Quarter (Call Someone Who Cares)
- High Cost of Low Living
- How Can I Miss You If You Won't Go Away?
- How Can You Believe Me When I Say I Love You, When You Know I've Been a Liar All My Life?
- How Come Your Dog Don't Bite Nobody but Me?
- I Bought the Shoes That Just Walked Out on Me
- I Don't Do Floors
- I Don't Know Whether to Kill Myself or Go Bowling
- I Fell for Her, She Fell for Him, and He Fell for Me
- I Gave Her My Heart and a Diamond, and She Clubbed Me with a Spade
- I Got Through Everything but the Door
- I Guess I Had Your Leavin' Coming
- I Keep Forgettin' I Forgot About You

(cont. on next page)

8.1 (continued)

- I Sent Her Artificial Flowers for Her Artificial Love
- I Would Have Wrote You a Letter, but I Couldn't Spell Yuck!
- If Love Were Oil, I'd Be a Quart Low
- If She Hadn't Been So Good Lookin', I Might Have Seen the Train
- I'm Just a Bug on the Windshield of Life
- Is It Cold in Here, or Is It Just You?
- My Wife Ran Off with My Best Friend, and I Sure Do Miss Him
- Occasional Wife
- Overlonely and Underkissed
- Redneck Martians Stole My Baby
- Refried Dreams
- She Made Toothpicks out of the Timber of My Heart
- The Pint of No Return
- They May Put Me in Prison, but They Can't Stop My Face from Breakin' Out
- Train Wreck of Emotion
- Walk Out Backwards Slowly So I'll Think You're Walking In
- You Can't Have Your Kate and Edith Too
- You Done Stomped on My Heart (and You Mashed That Sucker Flat)
- You Were Only a Splinter as I Slid Down the Banister of Life
- You're Out of Step (with the Beat of My Heart)

After completing the exercise in Figure 8.1, students can brainstorm verbal images or bring in different song lyrics to create different moods. Instead of the angst of love gone awry, which seems to be the fate of all country-song romances, they can paint alternate verbal pictures of love and other emotions. The questions to teachers and students are: How do you *choose* to feel? Whose hand is on the radio dial or CD player? Make informed selections wisely.

Our Song

Music has a way of attaching itself to emotional events in our lives. Hearing the song that played during your first slow dance, for instance, or selections from your wedding, can almost instantly transport you back to the special time you heard them and to the emotions you felt at that time (see Figure 8.2).

8.2 Pause and Apply

Make a list of songs with memorable lyrics that touch your heart. Try to remember the situation or event with which you associate each song. Pause to savor the memory.

Advertisers are acutely aware of this phenomenon and select music accordingly. As Tom Mucciolo revealed in his session at the 2002 Presentations Conference, advertising campaigns often will decide on a target audience and, to create nostalgia, incorporate hit music from when that demographic was 15 years old. Pay attention to television ads, particularly those that use a nostalgia-evoking sepia tint.[6] If you recognize the music, you are the target audience! We can get mad at advertisers who manipulate us, or we can gladly adopt their most effective techniques to achieve our own objectives. In this case, we can remember songs that made us happy, and we can create new associations and build up an invaluable collection of instant mood elevators—giving new meaning to the term "elevator music."

Words That Hurt

The old saying "Sticks and stones may break my bones, but words can never hurt me" has finally proven untrue. According to the *Journal of Women's Health and Gender-Based Medicine*, words can be very painful indeed:

> The department of anthropology at the University of Connecticut studied the emotional state of a group of working women of different

> cultural backgrounds. The study found that those women who were routinely subjected to insults and demeaning remarks were 85 times more likely to be clinically depressed than those who were spoken to favorably and with encouragement.[7]

If you are currently working in a classroom, try displaying the words "Kindness spoken here" atop the entry door. Consider writing those words in every language spoken by your students.

And Now a Word from Your Biggest Critic

Who is the most critical person in your life? Your mother? Father? Older sibling? Boss? Spouse? Kids? All of the above? Use the two columns in Figure 8.3 to tally all the criticism you receive on a given day. Place a check for every instance of self-criticism on the left, and one for every time you're criticized by others on the right. Count "constructive" criticism as well—as social anthropologist Jennifer James says, "Constructive criticism is just a slug in a tuxedo." And make sure to include those nagging self-reprisals: "Should have," "Ought to," "If only," etc. They're slugs too, every one of them.

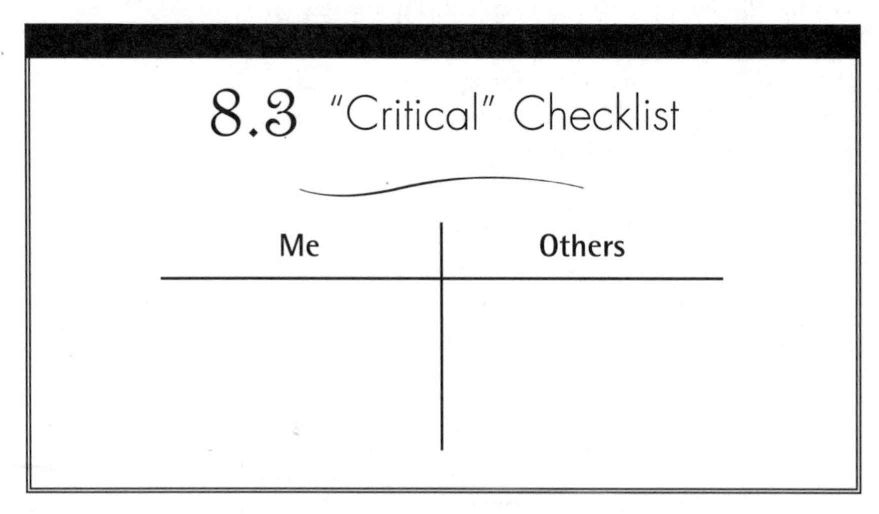

8.3 "Critical" Checklist

Me	Others

At the end of the day, add up the tally marks. Which column has the most marks? Are you surprised? If the tally marks could be changed to all positive comments in just *one* of the columns, which one do you think would have more impact on how you felt about yourself by the end of the day?

Self-Talk: Take It to the Bank

Imagine a fantasy in which your fairy godmother gives you an infinite supply of $1,000 checks. If you are like most people with house and car payments, a little credit card debt, and elderly parents or college-bound children to support, you might even take a few days off work to stay home and write checks. But there's more. In this fantasy world, you can put these checks into your bank account, either as credits or as debits. Would you take time off work to put the $1,000 checks into the bank as debits? Millions of us do. That time is called "sick leave."

When we talk to ourselves, in a very real sense we "charge" our bodies with either sickness (debits) or health (credits). Comments with a positive emotional charge energize and enrich our lives and put resources into our reserve account; comments with a negative emotional charge drain us and leave us vulnerable to every "virus" that comes along. There is no "neutral" column in Figure 8.3. You have to decide where to make the entries.

Verbal Antidotes

In *Feelings Buried Alive Never Die*, Karol Truman lists 759 commonly used negative "feeling" words, each with several powerful antidotes.[8] For example, consider one of our most basic negative emotions, *fear*. Truman calls it "the dark room where all the negatives are developed."[9] Conventional wisdom postulates that the antidote for fear is *courage*. In many cases, courage *does* triumph over fear. But courage rarely sustains itself unless it is backed by an even more powerful emotion: *love*. Ultimately, the opposite of fear is love.

A second power word, which shows up 100 times in Truman's "positive" feelings column, is *forgiveness*. Truman says that if we consistently forgive ourselves and others, we can defuse a hundred negative emotions, including anger, animosity, bitterness, defensiveness, disappointment, hostility, guilt, hurt, irritation, malice, pettiness, punishment, rage, regret, remorse, and resentment. You made a mistake? Learn from it, be thankful for the lesson, and move on. As our friend Joani puts it: "Life is full of lessons. Make mine quick!"

We propose a third power word: *called*. Educators, like ministers, often feel called to their profession. This sense of purpose—the passion for the cause—is the positive charge that energizes and keeps us going under difficult circumstances.

Those words—*love, forgiveness, called*—can ring true in all of our lives. A heart filled by those words can transform a stressed-out human into a resourceful saint. Pause for a moment and do the exercise in Figure 8.4.

8.4 Pause and Apply

Love, forgiveness, called. Think of the life of Mother Teresa. Reflect on how each of these words played out in her life as well as in yours. Savor the privilege and power of these emotional states.

Make your own list of power words. Look for appropriate opportunities to say them to yourself and to the people around you.

Your Heart Knows

In an August 2000 workshop, Richard Bolles pointed out that our hearts know the words we want to hear. He shared with us that even though he is a writer, he could never write about nuclear bomb parts, say, or medieval instruments of torture. It's his passion for a specific content area—career and mission planning—that inspires his gift for written expression.

To bring this point home in the seminar, Dick gave us a wonderful resource: *The Random House Webster's Word Menu.* This book—a combination dictionary, thesaurus, and almanac—organizes language by subject matter rather than by the traditional, decontextualized, alphabetical listing. Dick invited us to leaf through the book and find pages that contained words we would want to hear at work on a daily basis.

We started with the "Science and Technology" section. While words like "CPU," "computer," and "RAM" were familiar, they weren't particularly inspiring. So we moved on to "Institutions: Social Sciences: Education." Again the terms were very familiar, and some even tugged at the heartstrings. But it was upon reading the words listed under "The Human Condition: Faith: Truth, Wisdom, and Spiritual Attainment" that involuntary tears started pouring down our cheeks. Words like *awe*, *forgiveness*, *grace*, *harmony*, *numinous*, *peace*, *radiance*, *splendor*, and *vision* felt like a calling.

We came out of the exercise knowing that the content of our lessons, presentations, and books is less likely to be science and technology than ways to improve the human condition. There is no right or wrong answer in the *Word Menu* book; it is simply a tool for identifying your highest calling. As this calling lights your life's path, it also dispels the darkness. Stress, fear, resentment, anxiety—all these negative emotions are replaced by peace and a sense of certitude and abundance.

In a Heartbeat

While we're on the topic of good vibrations, it's time to consider the human heart. Though people have long believed that the brain controlled most of our physiological functioning, researchers have recently discovered that the heart is far more centrally involved in body regulation than the brain, and that there are far more ascending signals from the heart to the brain than there are descending signals from the brain to the heart.[10]

Much of this research has been conducted or collected by the Institute of HeartMath.[11] The institute has taken these amazing findings and applied them with remarkable results to schools, police departments, corporations, and even individuals. We've had the pleasure of learning about the institute's research as frequent guests at its facilities in Boulder Creek, California.

There are basically two kinds of bioelectrical signals that emerge from the heart. One is called a *coherent* signal because it has a smooth, gently curving appearance, and its "message" to the brain is that the heart is in a coherent, well-focused, smoothly functioning mode. The brain "hears" that message and initiates functions that reflect that state. The other kind of signal from the heart is *incoherent*, jagged, and disjunct; its "message" is "Red Alert: prepare to panic!" The brain "hears" that message and issues orders to support it.[12]

It is no accident that each of these signals from the heart has only one broad kind of emotional content connected with it. When we ask in our workshops what kind of emotional content people might suppose is carried in an incoherent signal, the responses include fear, anger, anxiety, frustration, guilt, shame, and depression. All of these are correct. An incoherent signal is always associated with emotions we customarily refer to as negative; conversely, a coherent signal is always associated with positive emotions such as love, appreciation, caring, and compassion.[13]

We are left with the profound understanding that negative emotions and their incoherent signals impair body and brain functioning, whereas coherent signals accompanied by positive emotions greatly enhance them.

Far Out

The brain and the heart both have electromagnetic fields that can be detected with an instrument called a magnometer. The brain's electromagnetic field can be measured with this instrument at a distance of roughly two inches away from the body. The heart's electromagnetic field, on the other hand, is far more powerful and can be detected at distances of *10 to 15 feet away from the body!* Because the electromagnetic field carries with it an emotional content, we all quite literally effect one another's vibrations—good or otherwise.[14] What implications does this have for schools? Imagine a teacher standing in the middle of a 30-foot by 30-foot classroom. The electromagnetic field emanating from that teacher spreads 10 to 15 feet in every direction. How do you think the class atmosphere is impacted by the teacher's emotional state?

Feeling Good

HeartMath's research led the organization to develop specific approaches to create and hold positive emotion in the heart consciously, in such a way as to allow the feeling to generate physiological and emotional responses of well-being and peak performance. We think there is a profound elegance to the HeartMath research, which reaffirms what we've always sensed in our own hearts: emotions that make us *feel* good actually *do* us great good. We may have thought this was merely poetic metaphor; now we find that life imitates poetry.

9

Power and Purpose

In the end, this is a book about nothing.

Reactions to stressors are real enough, both emotionally and physiologically. But, ironically, these reactions—from slackened performance at best, to sudden death at worst—all occur because of something that isn't even there. Stress is not the presence of something; quite the contrary, it is the absence of something.

Permit us to illustrate this important distinction with a familiar example. What is the opposite of light? Dark, of course. But what if we asked you to go get some more "dark" and put it in the room you're in right now? You couldn't do it. You can increase the light in the room—add more light fixtures, put in brighter bulbs—but you can't add more dark. The only way to increase darkness is to decrease light. Dark is not the presence of something; it is the absence of light.

Similarly, stress is not the presence of some objective reality, but rather the absence of resourcefulness. There are no ways to increase stress—only ways to decrease our ability to use our personal resources, even though they are always present. We cannot go get more of something called "stress." We can only impose or fail to remove limitations on our capacity to deal with life.

Stress is rife with ironies. Among them is the fact that as our ability to access resources decreases, circumstances that demand resources from us seem to increase. In other words, we get back exactly what we subconsciously believe to be true of ourselves. If we believe that our capabilities are limited, we draw to ourselves situations that support that belief. As those situations arise, they in turn reinforce what we believe about our inadequacies (e.g., "See? I knew I couldn't deal with this kind of thing").

It's not that the world has anything personal against us, though that's certainly how it looks; it's just that beliefs create expectations, becoming a kind of "thermostat" that limits our performance to where our attitude is "set." For example, if you believe you're terrible at keeping track of your finances, you manifest an attitude that is "set" at a certain threshold of patience and expectation; when you sit down to balance your checkbook, your attitudinal thermostat reminds you that you have no aptitude for this task and automatically restricts your patience. Errors are common when you believe that you won't get things right no matter what, so there's no point in trying to be accurate. Your subsequent poor performance is then submitted to your subconscious as yet more proof that your belief is correct. And so the vicious cycle, the self-fulfilling prophecy of negative beliefs, continues.

The good news about this is that exactly the same process is at work with empowering beliefs. And the thermostat can be totally disengaged. The most empowering beliefs know they have no upper limit, and so none is imposed.

Resources are "gated" by belief. For reasons even he doesn't fully understand, Lou has always believed that he could drive any kind of vehicle, regardless of whether he had ever driven it before. Back in college, he decided to apply for a job driving a bus, even though he'd never once sat in any bus driver's seat. During the job interview, the manager of the bus company asked him to do a test drive right then and there. With no time to prepare, Lou took the driver's seat and realized not only that he had to "know" immediately how to drive the bus but also that he had to look as though he'd been doing it for years. He still remembers the moment with awe:

> As I started up the bus, I felt a kind of vastly heightened intuition, drawing on resources I was not aware I had access to, that were now called into play because of my absolute belief in something that had no experiential reality. There would have been ample reason to believe that I was crazy even to try such a thing, that it was foolish, even dangerous. I recall instead feeling a wonderful power guiding me as I gracefully took the bus out of the parking lot, onto surface roads, and finally the freeway. Half an hour later, I was filling out the paperwork for my new job. Over the course of that job, I was considered one of the company's best drivers. I've had similar experiences over the years with many things other than driving.

> I still don't entirely know what comes over me that leads me to believe that I can do certain things. Of course, I have also given power to limitations by believing in them, and have seen the destructive results of such perverse 'faith.' Knowing now that we can choose to give power to any belief, healthy or otherwise, I've focused on empowering positive beliefs.

Out, Out, Damn Dark!

In the final analysis, this book is also about one very simple thought, most elegantly expressed in the poetry of a Chinese proverb: *It is better to light a candle than to curse the darkness*.

Our lives are too often spent quite literally cursing the darkness we know as stress: "I'd be able to see my way if it weren't for this wretched darkness!" But who of sound reasoning doesn't think to light a candle or turn on a flashlight if the power goes out at night? And what if there's a blackout around mealtime? Imagine yourself in the kitchen surrounded by all the resources that you could possibly need, but unable to see them. You fumble in the dark trying to do the job, getting increasingly frustrated, and finally become utterly dejected and resign yourself to failure and hunger. Metaphorically, we do this all the time.

In this book, we have purposely eschewed the term "stress management" to describe our approach to dealing with stress. We consider that term inaccurate. How do you "manage" darkness? You don't; you find or create light. Similarly, there is no way to "manage" stress—we can only increase our ability to draw upon resources. There are, of course, many things we can do to physically prepare ourselves to make the most of resources as we find them, and we've talked about most of those. But ultimately, dealing with stress means we stop cursing the darkness and light a candle.

In the darkest night, we can see the smallest flame. It takes only a little light in the human heart, only a slight movement toward the resources that abound within and around us, to begin to see our way out of stress. Each step builds on the last.

Multiple Levels of Meaning

If you ever want to try something new, different, and fun at a faculty meeting, come in, look around at the faces in the room, and ask, "*What is the meaning of this?*" You'll get a lot of quizzical stares, and some people might even consider the question.

There might be different answers on different levels. Experts in the field of Neuro-Linguistic Programming refer to "chunking up" and "chunking down" as ways of explaining how we discern meaning. For example, if you ask one person what a car means to him, he might mention chassis design, the internal combustion engine, the intricacy of moving parts, and the challenge of working on those parts. Ask another person, and he might say transportation, which to him means being able to go where he wants, the excitement of traveling to new places, and even the ability to control his own destiny. The first person is chunking down; the second person is chunking up. There is no qualitative judgment placed on up or down; neither is good or bad in and of itself. It just refers to the direction one's mind tends to go in considering the significance of any given thing. "Chunking up" sees the big picture; "chunking down" delves into details. Some people can and often do go both directions.

Let's return to our staff meeting. On one level, the "meaning" of the meeting could be its immediate agenda, such as new approaches to school technology. On another level, the meeting might signify a new opportunity for better budget control as the financial issues involved in technology integration are revisited from a new perspective. It could also mean changes in daily routine as new practices are created to handle the technology. On still another level, the meeting might mean a new opportunity for better bonding among staff members and a chance to use the issue of technology integration as a way to foster a renewed sense of community. To those with a broad range of concerns and perspectives, the meeting could simultaneously mean all these things and more.

The ability to discern greater levels of meaning in the flow of events and encounters in our lives doesn't make us more important than anyone else, but it does afford us greater personal resources and a much richer life experience. The challenge, though, is to perceive that higher truth consistently, without falling prey to any of the negative emotions that can distort and discolor our view of a typical day.

The Overlay of Shallow Meaning

In each of our minds there lurks an observer who watches all that we think and do. This observer keeps a scorecard on which it tallies every one of our thoughts and actions as either good or bad: You let that driver pull into traffic ahead of you? That's good. You're late for your meeting?

That's bad. You got the kids to school on time? Very good. You padded an expense account with a hundred dollars worth of personal stuff? Ooh, that's really bad.

The observer keeps score day in and day out, relentlessly. We aren't always aware of this internal judge, though sometimes we recognize it as the voice of particular people from our lives, past or present. (To this day, Lynell can't see herself in the mirror without hearing her mother ask, "Couldn't you have combed your hair?" On a more positive note, when she has the privilege of helping someone, Lynell always smiles and recalls the kind words of a teacher who recognized her "gift of encouragement.") Our overall feeling at any given point in the day—whether we're energized, content, fearful, angry, or whatever—is largely determined by the accumulated tally of good or bad marks amassed since we last took stock of our feelings. Our behavior is driven primarily by the desire to avoid negative marks and secondarily by a desire to score positive ones.

This incessant tallying—while it purports to be objective—actually occurs through an overlay that we've placed on the world around us. The overlay fits the general contours of reality so closely that we assume we perceive the world as it really is. When we see each other seated around a conference table at a staff meeting discussing technology integration, we are under the illusion that we're all having the same experience. But in reality we've each shaped our own individual overlays to match our own beliefs and assumptions about ourselves and the world. We never see a truly objective reality; every person in the faculty meeting is having a distinctly different experience. As the ancient wisdom goes, "We see the world not as it is, but as we are." Our overlays are screens through which we determine the value of ourselves and others. These determinations have little basis in reality, and therefore are almost always wrong. Our running checklist of good and bad has very little real meaning in the end because its evaluation of experience is perceived through erroneous overlays. Yet we base most of our emotional state on this type of evaluation.

This brings us to a critically important question: If our evaluations of good and bad are subjectively skewed, then what do good and bad really mean? Is there such a thing as objective, absolute good and bad? How would we know? How do we find true meaning?

The Power of Purpose

The best way we know of to explore true meaning and tap our inner resourcefulness is to understand the power of purpose. A sense of purpose ignites an imperishable flame that only grows in light and strength. *Significance, meaning, purpose*—these terms refer to a perceptual function of the human spirit.

We are sometimes asked why we focus so much on matters of the heart and spirit in education when there are so many pressing practical needs. We reply that the true *purpose* of education is fundamentally to empower and enrich the human heart. What does it profit a teacher to gain a mind but lose a heart? Clearly, the practical curricula of learning are critically important, but no more so than is fostering a loving and enlightened heart. We develop our greatest capacity for love by cultivating the broadest sense of purpose on the broadest levels we can find in ourselves (because we see the world as we are) and thereby in our students.

Clues to Purpose

Every once in a while, science becomes downright poetic. Some years ago, Professor Michael Grant at the University of Colorado at Boulder discovered the largest living organism on earth: a grove of aspen trees. This grove, which Grant and his team named Pando (Latin for "I spread"), grows in southern Utah in the form of thousands of aspens stretching for hundreds of miles. Above ground, the grove appears to comprise individual trees; however, Grant discovered that the trees all share one single root system.[1]

We believe that Pando offers a wonderful and accurate metaphor for humanity: one people, in many places, yet all connected at the root level. This connection plays out in life as a collective and individual desire for unity and wholeness, an inner realization that true purpose will always foster growth and well-being among *all* living beings, rather than enriching certain members at the expense of others.

The terrorists who flew planes into the World Trade Center believed they were following the will of a higher power that commanded them to destroy life. History is woefully full of such incidents. These people saw the world not as it is, but as they were. The highest challenge facing us all at the broadest level is to understand that we are not separate—what harms one, harms all. This same principle applies to daily life, especially in learning environments and places where we serve as role models, such as the home, the community, and most poignantly, the classroom. We discover true meaning and fulfillment when our lives are dedicated to serving the best interests of *every* life.

The What-How-Why Model

In her earlier work, Lynell pioneered a triune model for evaluating work. Previously, many people had considered it important to evaluate the "what" and the "how" of things: let's see *what* you've done (e.g., how original and well developed your concept is) and let's see *how* well you've done it (e.g., the level of craftsmanship). While teaching a design course at Stanford University, David Thornburg improved on the what-how model by making it multiplicative. He assigned values of 0 to 10 for each aspect of a work and, in grading his students, multiplied the figures together rather than adding them. Let's say, for instance, that a student delivered a brilliant presentation of poorly developed content. In such a case, the student might get a 10 on the "how" (technique) but score a 0 on the "what" (content). The total score, then, would not be 10 (10 plus 0), as it would be under an additive model, but 0 (10 times 0).

Lynell added a third criterion to David's approach: the "why" element. In other words, she proposed evaluating the intent behind the work in addition to the technique and the content. What were the students trying to achieve? How well did they accomplish their purpose? Did their presentation connect with the other students and inspire them to change an opinion or a point of view? Did it inform them of something that would make a difference in their lives? Did it transform their thinking? Touch their hearts? Call them to action?

The point of Lynell's triune model is to help us remember that whenever we do things in life, we must take into account not only *what* we're doing and *how* we're doing it, but also—and most importantly—*why* we're doing it. Imagine, for example, if everyone in the staff meeting we mentioned earlier had the model in Figure 9.1 in front of them.

9.1 Triune Model of Evaluation

Staff Meeting on Technology Integration		
What	How	Why

Here the issues of *what* and *how* are clear, and they can be given scores of 0 to 10 based on efficacy, cost, and a host of other practical concerns. When considering *why*, the score should be based on the answer to the following question: "How well does this meeting serve the best interests of everyone concerned?" If the event harms anyone, the score is 0. If it meets the needs of only a small percentage of people, the score might be as low as 1 or 2. If the plan is exceptional and everyone really does benefit, the score might be 9 or even 10. Remember that the model is multiplicative: don't just add the scores from all three columns. Multiply them together.

The "Why" column of the chart in Figure 9.1 reminds us that the purpose of all endeavors is predicated on how they serve all the people involved. Is it unrealistic to think that complex issues such as those facing education can be seriously addressed by trying, perhaps in vain, to help everyone? We don't think so. (And anyway, trying to *help* everyone is not the same thing as trying to *please* everyone.) The very terms "impractical" and "unrealistic" are attitudinal thermostat settings, and they limit us to the results they expect. But even if fulfilling a larger purpose really were impossible, the effort to do so is never a wasted one; the debate on what constitutes the best for all is itself worth the effort.

Of course, any such debate quickly reveals that people have wildly differing opinions on what is the "best for all." Faced with these differences, most people will abandon the discussion and start looking for ways to accommodate the disparate interests of all concerned. While this can sometimes be useful, more often than not it just ends up lowering the thermostat setting for the group as a whole. It has no more basis in reality than does any other limiting belief.

Power vs. Force

Few people have been able to demonstrate the strata of human attitudes more profoundly than David Hawkins. In his 1995 book *Power vs. Force: The Hidden Determinants of Human Behavior,* Hawkins provides a map of the human consciousness that depicts what Lynell calls a "spreadsheet" of humanity.[2] The map includes 17 levels of consciousness arranged on a logarithmic scale of 0 to 1,000. As part of the research for his doctoral thesis that subsequently led to the publishing of *Power vs. Force*, Hawkins conducted over 250,000 experiments using applied kinesiology to establish the levels on the Map of Consciousnesss. (Refer to Chapter 7 for a discussion of this technique.) The scale is divided into two broad categories: levels of consciousness that register below 200 on the logarithmic scale are characterized as operating from "force," whereas those that register above 200 operate from "power."

As Hawkins explains, people who play out their lives at levels below 200 on the scale are primarily motivated by self-survival, although even this primal motive is lacking in the zones of apathy and shame, which have largely surrendered the hope of survival (at least emotionally). The levels of fear and anger are characterized by an egocentric drive for personal survival; courage expands the motivation to include the survival of others as well. As one crosses the demarcation point between force and power states, the well-being of others becomes increasingly important. At consciousness levels above 500, the happiness of others emerges as the essential motivation.[3]

Consciousness levels below 200 must use force to maintain themselves; they constantly need replenishing, typically at the cost of other people's energies. Consciousness levels above 200, on the other hand, sustain energy and energize other people as well. The very terms "power" and "force" reflect the positive and negative aspects of the levels they describe. In education, for example, we see the *empowerment* of students and teachers versus to the *enforcement* of systems, policies, and procedures that meet resistance on the part of students and drain the energy, dreams, and creativity of staff.

Although further discussion of *Power vs. Force* is beyond the purview of this book, we highly recommend it as a resource to educators who want to operate more compassionately, think more positively, and dedicate themselves to opening the gateways to growth and development for themselves and their students.

Linear and Nonlinear Perspectives

We live simultaneously in two worlds: the "linear/physical" world and the "nonlinear/emotional"—some might say "spiritual"—world.

In the linear world, things are always in motion, progressing from point to point and from past to future in a clear logical sequence. This is the world of science and academia—fields that focus on methodical case-building, exactitude, and ducks neatly arranged in their prescribed rows. Everything here—from flowers to government bonds—needs time to grow and mature. There is little rest: tranquility can only be experienced between periods of distinct motion. Most of us believe we can navigate and even control the linear with reason and logic. And because it's the world we perceive through our physical senses, it's easy to believe it's the one we primarily inhabit.

But it's not. Although we live *through* the linear world, our primary world is nonlinear. This is the world of emotions, the realm of artists, musicians, and, for computer buffs, hyperlinked text and graphics. Here, the heart gives direction, encouraging us to leap from point A to point X without a care in the world for how we got there. There is no frantic scurrying in this world. All is tranquil; everything is at peace. In the nonlinear world, we experience courage, willingness, acceptance, joy, and love. We don't grow into such feelings; rather, we remove blocks within us that keep us from experiencing them to our fullest capacity. We excavate this capacity through an archeology of the spirit, digging through layers of hurt, self-doubt, and limitations.

There is a simple way to compare the natures of the linear and nonlinear worlds. In the linear world, most people say they want more money. That is a linear-world desire. But if we ask ourselves *why* we want more money, we might answer that we want to buy better things for our families, or be able to do things we can't do now, or get out of debt. For every such answer, we could ask ourselves again: *why? Why* do we want better things for our families? *Why* do we want to do things we feel we can't do now? *Why* do we want to get out of debt? Well, we might respond, to be a good provider, to have more fun and accomplish more, to be free. *Why?* If we keep asking, we will reach a point of understanding that the true impetus behind wanting more money ultimately reveals a desire of the heart, of feeling, of the need to be fulfilled in a nonlinear way. At this point we go beyond the reasons of the linear world to the reasoning of the nonlinear world, where we can experience the heart of what it means to be a fulfilled human being. As the 17th-century French philosopher Blaise Pascal put it, "*Le coeur a des raisons que la raison ne connaît pas*" (The heart has reasons that reason does not comprehend). While Pascal's phrase is most commonly used today in columns to the lovelorn, it could just as well serve as the rallying cry of many of us who were called into the education profession. The motivation for teaching is inherently a sense of purpose, a kind of *mission*, if you will, where the *why* (reaching, encouraging, and empowering every learner) is every bit as important as the *what* (curriculum) and the *how* (methodology). In the end, as all teachers know from joyous experience, it's the *why* of what we do that always leads us back to the highest aspirations of the human heart.

The Global Parking Lot

We closed the first chapter of this book with an exercise asking you to contemplate the lives of people coming and going in a school parking lot. Let's revisit the same exercise now, only this time on a global scale (see Figure 9.2).

How well you succeed in this effort is less significant than the intention invested in it. Through this exercise, you—and, through you, your students—can arrive at a fuller, deeper understanding of yourself and your world. Purpose becomes increasingly self-evident and life more meaningful

9.2 Pause and Apply

When you have some free time, go to a large shopping center or any other place where a lot of people come and go. Find an area nearby where you can sit and watch the ebb and flow of people and cars. Watch the people as they pass and try to imagine what might be going on in their lives at this moment. Here are some examples:

- That lady there, getting out of the white Taurus with her young daughter wearing sweats. She's in a hurry, with an anxious look on her face. Maybe she's late getting her daughter to dance class and they just had an argument about it in the car. The daughter is frustrated, trying to get her mother to understand how much the class means to her, and yet her mother is always late.
- That young couple, arm in arm, walking out of Sears with a large box. They've been married now maybe three months. They just bought a new microwave for their new home! It's something so small, yet so special. You can just see their love for each other in their faces, as well as their love for the microwave, which instantly acquires a meaning it might never have had outside of this context.
- The elderly gentlemen struggling to park his tiny car in a space wide enough to park a large truck. Why is he even still driving? His life boundaries have narrowed so much that he now strains to do something that would have been effortless just a few years ago! Maybe he's here to buy a gift for his wife of 58 years; suddenly, and on a different level completely, his boundaries achieve a breadth many of us would envy.

Do this for a couple of hours, person after person. Then contemplate how small a slice of life this represents. The same traffic of life is playing out at other shopping centers, at office and medical complexes, neighborhood after neighborhood, city after city, country after country. So many lives in motion, interacting with so many others! Such an infinite number of circumstances! How different these lives could be if they all redirected their energies to perceive the Big Picture. By getting a sense of the pulse of the universe, you can better appreciate the mercurial flow of life and meaning.

and compassionate. Stress can no more be sustained in such a state than darkness can linger in a brightly lit room.

The Call to Wake Up

In Chapter 1 of this book we played with the idea of prying your body from sleep. We end the book now with another kind of wake-up call: to awaken your hopes and desires from elusive dreams. We find it quite telling that people speak of wishes as "dreams," as though they could conceive of them only while sleeping. Yet of all the dreams we hold dear, none is more significant than the dream of someday awakening to our full potential, our highest calling, and our truest selves.

Throughout this book, we have proposed resourcefulness as the best antidote to stress. The best resource we can leave you with is a vast chunking up of the concept of the wake-up call. True living isn't something we can do in our sleep. Morning has broken. Time to enlighten up and join us in a good stretch . . .

Endnotes

Chapter 1

1. Putnam, C., & Sherrill, B. (Writers). (1967). My elusive dreams. Nashville, TN: Tree Music Publishing Corporation.
2. Csikszentmihalyi, M. (1990). *Flow: The psychology of optimal experience*. New York: Harper & Row.
3. Rogers, A. (1996, July 22). Zen and the art of Olympic success. *Newsweek*, 35.
4. Hobson, J. A., & Leonard, J. A. (2001). *Out of its mind: Psychiatry in crisis—A call for reform*. Cambridge, MA: Perseus.
5. Life Extension Foundation [Web site]. (2002). Available: http://www.lef.org
6. American Heart Association [Web site]. (2002). Heart & stroke encyclopedia. Available: http://www.americanheart.org/presenter.jhtml?identifier=10000056
7. Whole Health Discount Center [Web site]. (2002). Available: www.health-pages.com/se/
8. Amen, D. (2001, May 14). [KCBS-AM radio interview]. San Francisco, CA.
9. Lark, S. M. (2001). *Dr. Lark's natural prescription for stress and anxiety*. Potomac, MD: Phillips Health.
10. Ibid.
11. Handy, C. (1994). *The age of paradox*. Cambridge, MA: Harvard Business School Press.

Chapter 2

1. David, J. (n.d.). Job stress can be a killer—literally [Online article]. Available: http://www.stybelpeabody.com/ideastress.htm
2. Rosch, P. J. (1991, May). Job stress: America's leading adult health problem. *USA Magazine*.
3. Wayne, D. (1998, February). Reactions to stress [Online article].
4. Eysenck, H. J. (1988). Personality, stress, and cancer: Prediction and prophylaxis. *British Journal of Medical Psychology, 61*, 57–75.
5. Ibid.
6. Allison, T. G., Williams, D. E., Miller, T. D., Pateen, C. A., Bailey, K. R., Squires, R. W., & Gau, G. T. (1995). Medical and economic costs of psychological distress in patients with coronary artery disease. *Mayo Clinic Proceedings, 70*, 734–742.

7. Childre, D., & Martin, H. (1999). *The HeartMath solution*. San Francisco: HarperCollins Publishers.
8. Chudler, E. (2002). The autonomic nervous system. *Neuroscience for kids* [Web site]. Available: http://faculty.washington.edu/chudler/auto.html
9. ANSAR Group, Inc. (2002). Autonomic nervous system physiology [Web site]. Available: http://ansargroupinc.com/page5.html
10. Childre, D. (1998). *Freeze Frame: One-minute stress management*. Boulder Creek, CA: Planetary Publishers.
11. McEwen, B., & Krahn, D. (1999, November). The response to stress [Online article]. Available: http://www.thedoctorwillseeyounow.com/articles/behavior/stress_3
12. Ritter, M. (1998, April 15). Study links hormone, memory loss. *Seattle Times*.
13. Kugler, H. (2000, October). Science notes. *Journal of Longevity*.
14. Stonaker, L. (2002, October 17). API test scores rise; target rate drops. *San Jose Mercury News*.
15. Khalsa, D. S., & Stauth, C. (1997). *Brain longevity*. New York: Warner Books.
16. Childre, D., & Martin, H. (1999). *The HeartMath solution*.
17. Ibid.
18. Ibid.
19. Childre, D. (1998). *Freeze Frame*.
20. Wilson, J. L. (2001). *Adrenal fatigue: The 21st-century stress syndrome*. Petaluma, CA: Smart Publications.
21. Kirsta, A. (1986). *The book of stress survival*. New York: Simon & Schuster.
22. Ibid.
23. Higgs, L. C. (1995). *Only angels can wing it*. Nashville: Thomas Nelson Publishers.
24. Ibid.

Chapter 3

1. Crace, J. (2002, January 15). Life after work? *The Guardian*. Available: http://education.guardian.co.uk/teachershortage/story/0,7348,632682,00.html
2. Ibid.
3. Anthony, T. (1999, September 28). Hurry, hurry, hurry! Step right up to the frantic 20th century! *The Topeka Capital-Journal*. Available: http://celebrate2000.cjonline.com/stories/092899/tec_hurry928.shtml
4. Ibid.
5. Cantine, M. (2001, February). Virtual hilarity. *Reader's Digest*.
6. Mahoney, D., & Restak, R. (1998). *The longevity strategy*. New York: John Wiley & Sons.
7. Friedman, S. (1997). To do or not to do [Online article]. Available: www.FunnyScott.com>
8. Ibid.
9. Casey, K. (2000, March). Who has the most stress? *Ladies Home Journal*.

10. Rechtschaffen, S. (1999). Foreword. In D. Childre & H. Martin, *The HeartMath solution*. San Francisco: HarperCollins Publishers.
11. Goudey, P. (2000). *The unofficial guide to beating stress*. Foster City, CA: IDG Books Worldwide, Inc.
12. Desai, J. (2001, May). Stressed to the max. *San Jose Magazine*.

Chapter 5

1. Leider, R. J. (1997). *The power of purpose: Creating meaning in your life and work*. San Francisco: Berrett-Koehler Publishers, Inc.
2. Covey, S. R., Merrill, A. R., & Merrill, R. R. (1994). *First things first: To live, to love, to learn, to leave a legacy*. New York: Simon & Schuster.
3. Public Agenda. (2001, October). *Trying to stay ahead of the game: Superintendents and principals talk about school leadership*. New York: Author. Available: http://www.publicagenda.org/specials/leadership/leadership.htm
4. National Association of Secondary School Principals (2001, November 13). *Priorities and barriers in high school leadership: A survey of principals*. Reston, VA: Author. Available: http://www.principals.org/publicaffairs/pr_prncpl_srvy1101.html
5. Scherer, M. (2001, September). How and why standards can improve student achievement: A conversation with Robert J. Marzano. *Educational Leadership*.

Chapter 6

1. Kiyosaki, R. T., & Lechter, S. L. (1998). *Rich dad, poor dad: What the rich teach their kids about money—that the poor and middle class do not!* New York: Warner Books.
2. Smalling, D. (2001, April 1). Simplify your finances. *Bottom Line Personal*.

Chapter 7

1. Sartre, J. P. (1947). *Huis clos*. Paris: Editions Gallimard.
2. Lark, S. (2002, March). Surviving grief. *The Lark Letter*, 3.
3. Ibid., 5.
4. Truman, K. (2000). *Healing feelings . . . from our heart*. Las Vegas: Olympus Distributing.
5. Lucado, M. (2002, February). A palm full of mercy. *Decision*, 13.
6. Williams, R., & Lipton, B. (2001). *The biology of perception/The psychology of change* [Videotape]. Memphis: Spirit 2000 Inc.
7. Ibid.
8. Ibid.
9. Diamond, J. (1994). *Your body doesn't lie: Unlock the power of your natural energy!* New York: Warner Books.
10. Ibid.
11. Truman, K. (2000). *Healing feelings*.

12. Angelou, M. (2002, February). *Endure, dream, fail, survive*. Keynote address presented at the Presentations 2002 Conference, Atlanta.
13. Truman, K. (2000). *Healing feelings*.

Chapter 8

1. Doman, A., Leeds, J., & Minson, R. (2002). *The Listening Program training manual*. Ogden, UT: Advanced Brain Technologies.
2. Minson, R. (1994, Winter). Singing with the ear. *Connections*, 8(4), 94–95.
3. Doman, A., Leeds, J. P., and Minson, R. (2002). *Listening Program training manual*.
4. For more information on psychoacoustics, we recommend the following books, both of which are available for purchase at http://www.thepowerofsound.com:

   Leeds, J. (2001). *The power of sound: How to manage your personal soundscape for a vital, productive, and healthy life*. Rochester, VT: Healing Arts Press.

   Leeds, J. (1997). *Sonic alchemy*. Sausalito, CA: InnerSong Press.
5. Doman, A., Leeds, J. P., and Minson, R. (2002). *Listening Program training manual*.
6. For a discussion of the sepia tone, see Burmark, L. (2002). *Visual literacy: Learn to see, see to learn*. Arlington, VA: Association for Supervision and Curriculum Development.
7. Handwerker, W. P. (1999). Cultural diversity, stress, and depression: Working women in the Americas. *Journal of Women's Health and Gender-Based Medicine*, 8, 1303–1311.
8. Truman, K. (1991). *Feelings buried alive never die*. Las Vegas: Olympus Distributing.
9. Ibid., 113.
10. Please see the Institute of HeartMath Web site for more information. Available: http://www.heartmath.org
11. McCraty, R., Atkinson, M., & Tomasino, D. (2001). *Science of the heart: An overview of research conducted by the Institute of HeartMath*. Boulder Creek, CA: HeartMath Research Center.
12. Ibid., 16–18.
13. Rein, G., Atkinson, M., & McCraty, R. (1995, Summer). The physiological and psychological effects of compassion and anger. *Journal of Advancement in Medicine*, 8(2), 92–99.
14. McCraty, Atkinson, and Tomasino, *Science of the heart*, 20–21.

Chapter 9

1. The most massive living thing [Online article]. (2002, March 13). Available: http://www.extremescience.com/aspengrove.htm
2. Hawkins, D. R. (1998). *Power vs. force: The hidden determinants of human behavior*. Sedona, AZ: Veritas Publishing.
3. Ibid., 80.

Index

Note: Page numbers followed by *f* indicate figures.

About the Authors

Lynell Burmark and **Lou Fournier** are in frequent demand as presenters and trainers in stress abatement. Lynell is the author of the 2002 ASCD book, *Visual Literacy: Learn to See, See to Learn*; Lou has worked as a journalist and as a senior executive with education-technology companies. Together they are founders of VisionShift International as well as associates at the Illinois-based Thornburg Center for Professional Development. They can be reached via e-mail at lynellb@aol.com (Lynell) and louphonia@earthlink.net (Lou).